# SUPERVISORS IN ACTION

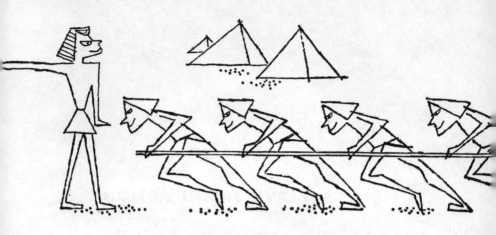

# SUPERVISORS IN ACTION

*Developing Your Skills in Managing People*

J. J. FAMULARO

*Drawings by A. S. H. Associates*

McGRAW-HILL BOOK COMPANY, INC.

*New York    Toronto    London    1961*

**VII**

19910

SUPERVISORS IN ACTION

*To Angela and Papa Joe*

# PREFACE

Almost everywhere you look, you see someone supervising someone else—whether in a textile plant in South Carolina, on a farm in Idaho, in an engineering office in California, in an insurance company in Hartford, on a new highway cutting its path across Ohio, in a mine hundreds of feet below the hills of West Virginia, or on Times Square in New York City where a dozen men or so may be planting new telephone lines. In our grand industrial and commercial design, there are hundreds of thousands of men and women each of whom is responsible for the job activities of one or more people. They are in every corner of your plant and in every corner of your office building. They are called section heads, leadmen, foremen, forewomen, assistant supervisors, section managers, floor managers, superintendents, department heads, assistant vice presidents, vice presidents, and, of course, presidents—to mention only some of the more popularly known titles. The list would be exhaustive if we included chief clerk, chief account-ant, chief engineer, etc. Collectively, they are called *supervisors* in this book, and they are responsible for the work done in jobs from basement to board room. This book is written for them. Its purpose is to take a look at the herculean management job of planning, or-ganizing, and controlling human resources—the job of managing people day by day.

With each passing year, the need for better employee-supervisor relations has become more and more impor-tant, and the need for more and more supervisors has become critical. There's no doubt in my mind that we will meet and satisfy both these needs. But we must plan for it, take action for it, and derive personal satisfaction from it.

What makes a successful supervisor? Hundreds of studies have been initiated in order to arrive at a satis-factory answer to this question. But when facts were accumulated, data analyzed, and conclusions drawn, still no final claim could be made about the universality of the findings. Yet we know there are people who are suc-cessful supervisors. If you, as a supervisor, are considered successful, it is because of a tripod of judgments: what your employees think of you, what your boss thinks of you, and what you think of yourself.

One of your prime duties is to get a specified amount of work accomplished in a specified amount of time.

But let's face it—your growth, your success, is not based on this alone. Your *employees* expect you to satisfy their individual needs, and your *superior* expects you to help him get his job done. And there are, of course, *your* own expectations and needs. Your ability to handle all three requirements means successful supervision. The successful supervisor has a sense of proportion about himself, his subordinates, and his superiors.

To paraphrase the words of Michaelangelo, *"Ancora imparo"* ("I'm still learning"), most supervisors know that one condition for being on top of their jobs is the attitude that *ancora impariamo* (we are still learning). Whatever joys or misgivings you get from these pages, I too humbly admit that *ancora imparo*. But it is my sincere hope that in this book you will find a suggestion, a thought, a statement, a different perspective, a new idea, or a fresh point of view about yourself, your employees, and the boss, any or all of which may increase your chances of greater success as supervisor.

As for the new supervisor, I hope the book will give him some idea of the job which faces him. For the experienced supervisor, I hope it will mean a newer and more challenging look at the people who keep him so busy for so many hours. For the student, my hope is that it will provide food for thought. The personnel man will understand my hope that it will help him come to grips with the supervisors, on whom so much depends. And for the training man, my hope is that he will not accept the *status quo* but will keep working and searching for improved methods, for stimulating improved supervision in and out of training rooms. For company officers who feel that people are not only their biggest problems but also their biggest assets, my hope is that, after reflecting the thoughts on these pages, they will emphasize the need for finding answers to many of the unsolved problems of supervisors, the key men in their organizations. For the reader, wherever you supervise, whomever you supervise: good luck! We need you.

In writing about the techniques and philosophy expressed in this book, I have relied primarily on my own practical experience. Naturally, however, there can be no doubt that my thinking has been influenced by the literature in the field, although in too general a way to permit of specific credits. Nor is it possible to acknowledge individually the valuable contributions that have come to me from my associates through the years. But two special expressions of gratitude must be made. Bernard H. Kinzer, Director of Employee Relations for the Columbia Gas System, was exceedingly helpful. In addition to reading the manuscript, he made many valuable criticisms and suggestions which helped shape this book. And without the cooperation of Joan Muessen, who gave so generously of her time, preparation of the book would have been quite impossible, for she helped plant these "seeds of supervision;" then, carefully and patiently, she tended their growth into manuscript form.

*J. J. Famularo*

# CONTENTS

# SUPERVISORS IN ACTION

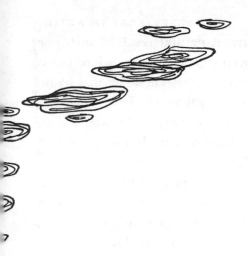

# 1

# COMMUNICATIONS

### *organizational blood cells*

Communications is the lifeblood of business. If we are to believe today what Mr. Coolidge said in 1925, that "The business of America is business," the development and maintenance of a good communications system is a modern cure for any case of business anemia. This is basic. It is the foundation on which this book is built. The new emphasis on communications in industry and business is not surprising. America's modern business continues to grow and expand by leaps and bounds, and

growing pains are many. A natural result of such phe-
nomenal growth has been the divergence of interests of
management and employee. Everyone hopes that by improving methods of communications impersonal corporate behavior can become personal and bridge the gap
between employees and management. Industry and business in our time, willingly or unwillingly, respect the.
growth of the labor-union movement. This in itself challenges management to accent communications, to vie
for the allegiance and attention of employees both of
which have been given to unions in large doses. No longer
is silence golden. No longer can misunderstandings fer-
ment in secret caves. Industrial and business pace setters
and their followers have made a sharp about-face. They
know that the wheels of progress will turn only as
rapidly and travel only as far as they can carry the con-
sent of the public—those millions of people who are
employees, stockholders, voters, consumers, suppliers,
neighbors, and friends. This about-face suggests that
American industry and business have admitted less proficiency in managing their people than in managing their
machines, manufacturing, and materials. So once again,
when it seemed as if the chips were down, American in-
genuity has accepted a challenge. In the face of growth,
change, and competition, a stronger and better way to
communicate has been the healthy result.

There are two distinct aspects to communications: getting through to people's minds and getting action from

these people. The objective in getting through involves not only the selection of words, actions, or symbols that convey our thoughts but also the consideration of how these same words, actions, or symbols will be interpreted. The objective in getting action is to influence people to achieve the goals we want. If action does not result, there has been no interchange of ideas; the communication process has broken down.

In this book, no single chapter is devoted to communications. Many are. In your job, communications, the bloodline of management-employee relations, means hiring, training, and sometimes reprimanding employees. It means giving orders, delegating, and always appraising employees. Communications in these managerial functions is making ideas common to yourself and one other person or more. In the following chapters, you are given a grasp of day-by-day communications between superior and subordinate and vice versa. They can't, of course, give you all the answers. Our basement philosophy tells us that in our jobs, the confusion, difficulties, and problems we meet are not as much with things as with those who work with things. The area of confusion, the amount of difficulty, and the number of your problems are directly related to how well you communicate. Some of the answers may be in the following pages.

Most of us are inclined to think of the communicative process as a formal procedure; for example, communication takes place during a formal appraisal program, a formal training program, a formal order giving. We cover these and other such areas in many of the following chapters, but there are many communications networks which are exceedingly less formal, and one of them deserves mention. One classic example is the office or plant grapevine which crawls over an organization like poison ivy. If you cut it, burn it, crush it, it sprouts and spreads all over again. Since its growth and development is not "structured" and follows different paths and directions, there is a variety of healthy vineyards in most corners of the company. People will talk; of this we can be sure. There are two schools of thought about the grapevine as a communicative process. Some say it is nothing more than a peddler of half-true gossip; others say that this "free and easy" talk *is* healthy and that it shows employees *do* have interest in what is going on around the company. Are grapevines planted in psychological beds? Yes, a grapevine may tell us how things stand, but most psychologists agree that it almost always allows employees to relieve deep emotional tensions. Why is gossip sparked so easily? What keeps it on the move? Its momentum is fed usually by antagonism, fear, and desire. You'll recognize this by recalling a jealous employee's murmur, "He quit because . . ."; the fearful employee's prognosis, "They won't need us anymore now that they're programming for the 7070 . . ."; and the hopeful employee whose prediction is completely unfounded when he informs other employees that "The vacation policy is changing to five weeks after . . ."

In controlling grapevine communications, successful supervisors will go up the line and *get the facts,* see that these facts are passed along the line by getting all their people together and explaining the situation, announce the bad news with the good, and refuse to answer questions about things of which they're not sure. Remember, each hour, each day, what *you say and don't say* will largely determine what your employees will feed to the grapevine.

Before starting our climb from basement to board room, let's think about what an up-and-coming manager, located in a sparkling new plant building near Chicago, Illinois, said to the author not too long ago. The author, impressed by the contemporary design of the building, the clean-cut landscaping, the many modern machines, the spacious office space, and the cozy, comfortable cafeteria, remarked how wonderful it must be to work in such a plant. The young manager said, "You're right, Joe, it is wonderful. The machines give me no trouble at all. Actually, Joe, I never had any trouble in this building until we let people in."

In your little or large plant, new or old office building, people are already in. We begin our story with your job and you.

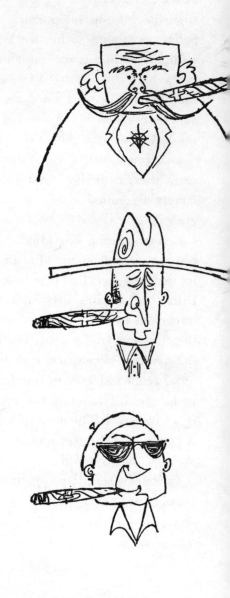

# 2

# YOUR JOB

## a full-sized view

In his essay on *Self-reliance,* Ralph Waldo Emerson said that "An institution is the lengthened shadow of one man." A few pages in the recent history of our great country give us illustrations. Look at the gigantic dynasties built by Rockefeller, Astor, Carnegie—dynasties entirely branded with the names of their master builders. At one time someone who talked about the New York Central was talking about Cornelius Vanderbilt. *The New York World* was Joseph Pulitzer, and what is now

United States Steel was Andrew Carnegie. The lengthened shadow is still with us, but in the last fifty or sixty
years a significant change in ownership has taken place.
"Industrial giants" are no longer owned and controlled
by one man. Instead, newly competitive advertising slo-
gans ring out, "Our company is owned by more than
200,000 stockholders." Today, the public, boards of directors, and top-management teams own, direct, and operate not only America's fifty largest corporations but
also the hundreds of medium- and smaller-sized organizations. As of last year, more than twelve million people
owned a share in American business. Proof of the disappearance of the dynasties is the disappearance of the
private estates which once covered thousands of neatly
trimmed acres on Long Island, in Newport, on Jekyll
Island, and on the sunny slopes of California.

In spite of the shift from private to public ownership,
the shadow of one man still strongly silhouettes itself
against the corporate background, perhaps not in the
eyes of Mr. and Mrs. John Q. Public, but in the eyes of
millions of employees throughout the country. Whose
shadow is this? Yours! The supervisor's! How many times
have you heard that "the supervisor *is* the company" to
the average employee, who may not know a member of
the board nor recognize the president of his company by
sight? Is it not true in your own organization that the
personality of a particular department is the reflection
of the man at the head of it? When you hear, "I'd like to

be in that department," aren't you also likely to hear, "I sure would like to work for that man"?

With all the technological and industrial advances since World War II, we are told that we are face to face with a world full of bigger and better changes, all of which create huge demands and opportunities for men with supervisory skills. These bigger and bluer skies mean that American industry will have to move quickly and take longer strides to meet the challenge ahead. Any wonder that in the past decade there has been and continues to be a mad scramble for the successful supervisor, the man who can manage and the man likely to become president? America faces a managerial crisis in the 1970s, said one executive at a recent conference.* He said the American economy would need 30 per cent more managers in the labor force in 1970 than today. These men will have

> ... to operate new industries, such as the atomic-energy industry ... to expand our present industrial capacity. The character of industrial change also increases our requirements. Decentralization, for example, will require additional managers. We may require a greater number of managers to operate American business abroad. But that is not all ... we shall need not only

* Charles W. V. Meares, "Management Development and the Coming Managerial Crisis," in *Industrial Relations Here and Now, A.M.A. Management Report No. 34,* AMA, New York, 1959, pp. 87–94. (Mr. Meares is vice president in charge of personnel, New York Life Insurance Company.)

more but better managers. They will require more education and better training.

Strange as it seems, supervisory skills are mostly the same wherever you go, wherever you are. Basically, the principles of supervision required to produce gyroscopes, guns, and gingerbread are the same. They are the same for service in the government, garages, or gas works. Skilled supervisors and men of management are needed everywhere. You've heard the expression "He's a born leader." Some few men may have been so luckily born, but by and large the majority of us must learn and practice such skills if we are to meet the challenge of the exciting future which awaits us.

### The new look of supervision

Not long ago, the boss was a dictator to be feared. He was an ogre, an economic despot who ruled with an iron hand, and he was sole owner of the superiority complex. Today's supervisor makes quite a contrast. The upsurge of power in the hands of labor organizations has been a major reason for such a marked difference. The threat of sit-down and sympathy strikes, slowdowns, and sabotage made employers realize that a new approach was needed in their relations with all employees. At the same time, especially since World War I, industrial psychology was beginning to bear fruit. This was clearly shown by one of the earliest and best-known experiments, which was made at the Western Electric Company. An important result of this study showed that employees who had become aware that they were being treated considerately had increased productivity. Other studies made more recently showed similar results. It was natural for supervisors and managers to conclude that it was better business to treat all employees fairly and squarely. The new look in supervision these days emphasizes the fact that management and labor are traveling the same road and therefore encounter the same signposts.

Before any attempt is made to analyze, evaluate, and improve your supervisory skills, an understanding of your job in the broad sense seems obvious and mandatory. Supervisors are a part of management. Development along managerial lines begins only after a supervisor has gained a clear concept of the responsibilities inherent in his job. When you were appointed a supervisor, you were put in a position to assume some of the responsibilities of management. Appointment alone does not make you a good leader. Often, supervisory development is retarded because someone lacks the understanding of the responsibilities of his job as supervisor. We should know, too, that responsibilities are delegated and that they may be increased or withdrawn at any time. Whether you're new in your job or celebrating your fifteenth anniversary as supervisor, retreat twenty paces or so and, as the painter views his total canvas, look at the major composition of your work. You should see:

1. *An area of purpose, policy, and program.* The ac-

tions taken by you and your employees must have definition and understanding. This is *what* you are doing and *why*. Policies steer and limit these actions, but at the same time they give employees a mutual road to follow. With a purpose and a policy, as supervisor you should also see a program—*how* and *when* the work will be done. Your program is a very tangible item in accomplishing your purpose via company policy.

2. *An area of working with and through people.* The productivity of your people may be in direct proportion with your ability to handle them. In order to perform your job, you are concerned with selecting, training, placing, promoting, and motivating the employees who are to accomplish the goals set up for your section. This is important outside your own department too—your relationships are interwoven with other supervisors, managers, and other levels of management and often with the public and community. All this means you have a tremendous sphere of influence with people.

3. *An area of problem solving.* Your capacity to perceive and analyze changing situations, varying conditions, and unusual circumstances must bring forth practical and basic solutions most of the time. You need not have an answer for everything, but your knowledge and influence should extend far enough so that a satisfactory conclusion may be obtained. One reason why you are where you are is that you've proved more right than wrong as problems presented themselves.

4. *An area of organizational structure,* not only of jobs to be performed, but of people to perform them successfully. The question "How will the work in my section be divided?" will have to be answered by identifying, defining, grouping, and assigning job duties. These job duties must be organized and maintained in order to accomplish what has been set forth. Organization is always present, whether it is defined in a finely detailed organizational chart or whether it is understood simply from who says what to whom. In either case, it is always with you. This organizational structure is superimposed on broad company policies and objectives, some of which may cramp your style, but it's part of your job to set up a proper section, department, or division.

5. *An area of knowing how to make what you've set up work.* This means rowing, not rocking the boat. Communicating ideas and objectives and getting your team to work together for a mutual and coordinated result adds up to know-how. In performing any task in any job, various actions must be taken. For example, in the area of employment, people could not be employed without contacting or interviewing actions. This is doing the job. As supervisor, your "doing" is made up of initiating and completing, researching and recommending, hiring and developing, training and correcting, to mention some of the actions you take. These actions are your responsible share of the total management goal. Your job is to keep in step with the music.

6. *An area of compliance and correction*. With all the activity in an organization, eventual success depends on the degree of disparity between what *should* be done and what *is* being done. As supervisor, you set up standards of performance. As supervisor, you keep yourself informed of the real performance through observation, reports, discussions, or control charts. As supervisor, you must evaluate the difference between what should be done and what is being done. You must be able to define this difference and determine what correction will be necessary to bring about full compliance between the two.

7. *An area of accepting accountability*. As a supervisor and part of management, your shoulders carry a share of the total organizational load. You and you alone are held accountable for this share. How willing are you to accept this accountability? Although authority may be delegated, you cannot delegate your own responsibility. You may delegate to a subordinate complete authority in handling a phase of your work, but the final responsibility is your own. With responsibility, there is always an obligation to handle problems arising therefrom. And doesn't responsibility gravitate to the man who proves himself capable of handling it?

It's a big order, isn't it? It's a lot of current, and probably you're wondering if your fuse can carry the load. Or perhaps you're counting the times your lights

blew out last month? Because it *is* a big order, your
company gave lots of time in deciding whether or not to
promote you to where you are. In their eyes, it's not a
matter of lights on, lights off. In their minds, your fuse
*can* carry the load. In understanding your job, is it not
true that in spite of all the advances in the social and
physical sciences of this push-button, jet, and missile age,
living these days can be strenuous and exasperating?
Competition grows keener, and more executive-suite
dramas are given live TV treatment. We not only worry
about the Russians and their ICBMs but also about the
company across the street and their new promotional
campaigns. It was bad enough that merit increases were
frozen after that two-point drop in stock, but now no
temporary help is available, and your schedule gets
tougher, and tougher.

### A new look at your qualities

A realistic approach in viewing your job also means
taking a look at some of the major qualities you need
(if you don't have them, then the qualities you need to
develop) if you are to fight off the pressures and carry
on with the big job you have to get done. What, then,
are some of these qualities?

1. *Give religion.* Most people want to follow, but who
and what they follow will determine the merit of the
group as a whole. People want and need inspiration. How
well you yourself believe in what you're doing, how you

transmit this feeling to your people, and how well this helps motivate them will determine the likelihood of success.

Giving religion means more than believing in yourself or in your job. It means believing in other people, your company, our economic and business ways of life, and our country. The company itself cannot breathe a word; its voice is through its people. You, in your job, as part of management, speak for the company. It is up to you to make the people you supervise feel they have hitched their wagons to a star.

2. *Love your work.* It's almost impossible to be a good supervisor and not take pride and joy in really doing a good job. Charles H. Malik, representative from Lebanon in the United Nations, said recently,*

> Sloppiness in workmanship is the curse of this age. People in the past slaved to produce perfect works of art much more than they do now. They are in a hurry today, they are practical, they have their minds much more on their rights and enjoyments than on their work, their hands shake, their eyes are moist, their minds are misty, and they do not love their work. Human relations in the industrial order will not improve until people, in place of worshipping themselves, worship the objective standard of excellence of their work. Again, what is wanted is pride in excellence and not in mere being!

* Charles H. Malik, *Human Relations and the Industrial Order*, AMA, New York, Feb. 27, 1959, 12pp.

3. *Have genuine enthusiasm for your team.* By his own enthusiastic attitude toward his unit, section, or department the successful supervisor instills in those under him a feeling of pride in their team and its achievements. A player on the New York Yankees once said that when you put on the Yankees' uniform, you grow three inches! The outstandingly high morale of the Yankees as a team was demonstrated by the fact that in the ten years between 1948 and 1958 they won nine pennants, yet only two players on the 1958 team were wearing the Yankees' uniform in 1948.

4. *Bring out the best in yourself and in other people.* It is generally accepted that with the right stimulus any of us will approach our jobs enthusiastically and perform beautifully. With indifferent or antagonistic supervision, our minds and bodies emaciate. Mail boy or vice president, the quality of one's performance swells or shrinks as a result of the kind of supervision he receives. Can there be any question that nations prosper, universities advance, and organizations succeed according to their ability to stimulate and bring out the best effort in each individual?

Is there any question in your mind that, if your subordinates sense restraint, feel limited, lack recognition, miss opportunities, and are treated unfairly, they will think and look elsewhere?

5. *Allow your employees to breathe while they work.* Many studies have shown that the poorer supervisors

hold a tight rein over the people they supervise. They breathe down their necks with frequent orders, volumi. nous complaints, and repetitious instructions on how *not* to do something. Most employees like to feel that they "know what they're doing" and prefer to move about their business on their own. The successful supervisor sets up broad goals and allows his employees sufficient procedural leeway to meet these goals. Often, a supervisor finds that the employee comes up with a better way of getting the job done than the supervisor would have thought of himself. It takes time to spell out each detail of the work to be performed and it takes additional time to follow through by watching every intricate step along the way. With such close supervision the employee feels he can't express himself; he follows the leader grudgingly, like the child who grimaces with each spoonful of spinach his mother crams down his throat. Close supervision is necessary in the training situation but, once the employee meets his "satisfactory level of performance," one certain way to get him to develop beyond this is to give him breathing space in his work environment. Loosen the reins and the majority of your employees will giddyap.

Here, then, are some of the broad areas of your job and some of the talents you will need to explore, discover, and develop. In spite of common-denominator supervisory skills, many able supervisors, entrusted with major management assignments, often achieve outstanding successes by using completely different methods. Some of these methods are covered in later chapters. But it is not usually possible to weigh the various ingredients of successful supervisors as you would their avoirdupois. We can be reasonably sure, though, that he who gains a full-sized view of the job before him and he who will do something to develop the skills and abilities inherent in a supervisor's job will be nearer to being the successful manager of people he wants to be.

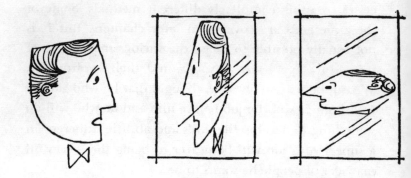

*3*

# YOURSELF

### *shadow or substance?*

In a recently published survey of supervisory opinion conducted by Glen Gardiner, publisher of *Management Information,* nine out of ten supervisors said their most challenging problem is the one of human relations. The survey indicates that although the supervisor's responsibility extends to cost control, quality, maintenance, and customer service, he realizes more than ever that he must get results through people and that stepped-up mechanization will magnify, rather than reduce, the importance of the human element. In this survey, 43 per cent of the supervisors polled seek solutions to problems of human behavior—how to understand people better, how to learn more about how to treat people as individuals, and the broader aspects of psychology. The survey suggests that the supervisor recognizes the importance of human relations but is often unsure in this area and looks to top management for help and guidance in solving these kinds of problems.

Understanding "what makes Sammy run" isn't easy. Individual needs and the devices concocted to satisfy these needs silver the mirror in which most people look at life. It's not easy for anyone to change his point of view, nor is it easy for him to see the other guy's perspective. Each of us appreciates our own attitudes and values—they're so comfortable. If an attitude or a value is agreeable and congruent with our own, we usually accept it. If it isn't, we often reject it. This is the stuff wars are made of. Look across the continent of Africa: How many of the values of Africans are you willing to accept? As George Kimble aptly said, "The darkest thing about Africa has always been our ignorance of it." * Or look around the corner on Main Street in a small Southern town. Tom Blair grew up in this town and now supervises a crew of twelve men who run and operate a mighty big compressor station in Nashville, Tennessee,

* George H. T. Kimble, "Africa Today: The Lifting Darkness," *The Reporter*, May 15, 1951.

for a mighty big pipeline outfit. Tom is the son of the local hardware dealer. He is at church every Sunday morning and is very active at church socials two evenings each week. Before he finished high school, he worked afternoons in the store and on Saturdays too. He worked hard and saved his small salary. Tom doesn't smoke and he doesn't drink. Tom is correct in every way. His crew at the compressor station are city slickers to him. They smoke and drink a little too much. One member of his crew hasn't been inside a church since the day he was married, fourteen years ago. No one can doubt that Tom's values are important to him, nor that they are Tom's values. But they daily crisscross other people's attitudes, and Tom is beginning to feel he's not the boss he should be. He asks himself: "Why am I different? Why do I think and feel as I do?" To answer these questions, Tom is going to have to find time to think about the way his beliefs and experiences affect his relationship with the members of his crew. He'll have to take a good hard look at himself. He'll have to dig deep, because understanding oneself is fundamental to an understanding of other people around you.

When a piece of machinery fails to do its job efficiently, a mechanic is always on hand to repair it quickly. There are thousands of maintenance men and equipment servicemen, and the payroll figures for them run into millions. The money spent for such repair is essential to industry, for without it there would be a loss of tens of thousands of dollars in investment, raw materials, and time. A piece of equipment which continually malfunctions is usually discarded. There are *men* in responsible jobs who fail to do their jobs efficiently, but there are no mechanics on call who hurry over to restore efficiency and set these men back on their feet. Like the piece of machinery, a man can malfunction repeatedly. Over a period of time his failures may multiply, and he too may be discarded. The company suffers a tremendous loss in training time and costs.

Tom Blair was carefully selected and promoted to his job. He has a good company history. But, like some other new supervisors, Tom hasn't realized that his one main problem lies in understanding other people by understanding himself. Tom's new job, a supervisor in charge of other men, has a new dimension, one that was not as important to him before his promotion. Before, he always got along fairly well—by himself. He worked mostly alone and wasn't in a position of expecting anything from anyone else. His values didn't get in the way. Psychologists say that much of our motivation is unconscious, and because our "defense mechanisms" work automatically, there are many aspects of our personalities that we aren't aware of. In the middle of a new set of circumstances, Tom, perhaps unknowingly, needed a new awareness of what makes Tommy tick. Ask yourself, as Tom surely will, how it may be possible to understand your personality and feelings better than you do.

### How high is your comfort index?

How often do you handle certain necessary aspects of your job which seem disagreeable to you, things your conscience won't permit you to do? Does your lack of action at these times result in self-punishment? Most people are not consciously aware of how strong their consciences may be. For example, in every group there's someone who has to be handled with kid gloves because he simply can't take any criticism. If he makes a mistake and is told about it, he pouts and becomes grossly unhappy. He feels inferior and guilty. In your job as supervisor, if you back down from correcting such an employee, examine your conscience. If you don't correct the employee, do you feel comfortable in not having done so?

Tom Blair had an oiler who occasionally drank on the job. The relations between other employees and the oiler were often ruffled, and the oiler never could perform his job efficiently on his inebrious days. Tom was growing more and more concerned over this, but he never could quite bring himself to the point where he could talk to the oiler and attempt to correct the situation. Sometimes, as Tom was shaving in the morning, he would look into the mirror and see the oiler and think, "Now, Andy, I know you had a good time last night, but you know this morning, compressor number 4 needed. . . ." Or, he would try this approach: "Gee, the gang had a good time, Andy, and it sure was a late party and everybody had a little too much—" Instead of his own half-shaven face, Tom would see the disgruntled look on Andy's face; he could almost hear Andy's retort and a case building up right then and there. He would decide to say nothing to Andy. After all, Andy was an old timer and had some pretty good qualities. Sure, Andy didn't always have his wits about him, but then he was always on the job, regardless of his condition.

Once he knew he would say nothing to Andy, Tom would begin to feel comfortable. But he didn't realize that his silent acceptance of Andy's condition on the job would result in frequent interference with a smoothly operating compressor station, Tom's pride and joy. The ill-at-ease state of Tom's conscience prevented him from properly evaluating and handling one of his important employees. He eased out of this situation, even though he knew that to face it and correct it would be to the advantage of the employee, other employees, and himself. If your comfort-seeking index is this high, delve into your conscience. Conscience is as expansive as outer space but responsible for many actions and feelings. It's important to know when your conscience will give and when it won't, what it tolerates and what it rejects.

### How high is your aggression quotient?

A strong aggressive drive can overcome inactivity that the conscience will not permit. Certain aggressive drives

in the personality of a supervisor can be desirable traits
—if only Tom, for example, had grabbed the bull by the
horns where Andy was concerned. These aggressive actions can be a real source of happiness and satisfaction
for yourself, your family, and your employees at work.
Your success in aggressive activity may be in the area of
volunteer work for the Boy Scouts, or a special fund-
raising campaign for the Kiwanis Club, or organization
work for the company bowling league, or a new time-
saving practice you started in the plant. It has been
said that all human beings have aggressive drives. The
amount of the drive varies from individual to individual,
but what must be taken into consideration is whether
or not something constructive is made with whatever
amount of drive is present. One way of learning more
about yourself is to watch these drives at work. One labor-
relations man very carefully evaluated the aggressive
drives of various union organizers and decided to bring
about the promotion of one of these men from organizer
to a key-spot manager's job where union-company relation was in need of help. The signs of aggressiveness that
cause trouble are not the constructive ones, but the tens
of little drives that provoke "local wars" at every turn.
You'll recognize them easily.

There's the practical joker, for example, who always
gets a laugh at someone else's expense. Behind this kind
of humor usually lurks a sharp blade of aggression, and
though there may be nothing wrong with the humorous

statement, take a look at the person at whom it was directed. Akin to the practical joker is the aper, the mimicker, the court jester. He's got the big boss's walk down pat and a department head's eloquent speech down to a tee. He's the little boy in the second grade who has drawn his teacher's portrait on the blackboard before she appears for class. Again, *who* is aped, *who* is mimicked? More little signs of aggression, but are they constructive? The supervisor of the stenographic department is known as Honest Nell because she insists on telling the truth, the whole truth, and nothing but the truth. Each morning, as each stenographer passes "the isolation booth," she remarks, "Mary, you look awful in that shade of blue." Or, "Gwen, you're gaining weight." Each supervisor, more than other employees has a natural chance to let loose with these unconstructive bits of aggression: a severe reprimand when a little mistake has been made, holding the reins so hard and fast, no fair deal in the distribution of work, taking it out on the same employee day in and day out, feeding the grapevine in his own section, and lashing a subordinate because of his own reaction to his superior. Analyze these actions and you'll get a better indication of your aggression quotient.

### How much action do management and employees need and expect of you?

Management people and employees can be very helpful to you in understanding yourself. They have set up a list of expectations which you should be aware of. At your supervisor's meetings, by direct contact with your superior, or by memo from a major department head, you are fairly well informed as to what the company expects: efficient production, high quality, cost control, minimum absenteeism, and low turnover. These standards of performance are universal, regardless of the geographical location, the industry or the plant, office, or factory in which you work. But you may not know that each day there are other expectations, many of which are unrequested, unspoken, written between the lines but pervade the atmosphere and surround you like ants on a hill.

Your management may want to know employee reaction about the Christmas party which didn't come off or the reaction to the new morning coffee break. They may want to know the reaction to a general 5 per cent wage increase or what the feeling is about the new time report. After a serious accident, Tom Blair's superior might have wondered why he was not made aware of Andy's problem. This kind of "no news" to the boss surely will result in bad news. You may follow a preplanned schedule of operations or a tight union contract, but where does it tell you how to handle your people? Some management expectations are in writing—you may have a manual on personnel relations, memoranda on approved procedures, and monthly quota targets—but nowhere are employee expectations listed. These may be and generally are more complicated. True, employee expectations may be listed in the union contract, but employees still have to look to you to put decisions into actions. Job seniority, promotions, layoffs, call-out pay, vacations, and overtime regulations may be spelled out in the contract, but where does it say how you are to handle new employees who have never worked before, or how to listen to the seriousness of a wife's illness, or how Junior can get a summer job? Where is Tom Blair's rule book for action to be taken with Andy? Did Tom have any idea of Andy's expectations, good or bad?

Elementary psychology teaches that most people act toward authority in the way they reacted toward authority in the home. Supervisor and father become synonymous. The young immature boy coming out of high school or trade school needs to lean on his first supervisor for plant rules and regulations. The supervisor must know what this new employee expects of him. Is it a matter of explaining the quantity of a day's work, information about a new piece of equipment, or the limits of discipline in the department? Perhaps employees expect you to listen to their troubles. Or perhaps they think *you* are the one to represent their views to your superiors. Do you think they want information from *you* about company plans for expansion, or do they have to wait to read about it in the local newspaper? Do they expect positive evaluation of their job performance or just a mere "You're getting along all right"? Do they want to be considered next in line for the next promotion, or do they expect an outsider to reap the harvest?

Do they expect commendation for a job well done or just to be handed another difficult assignment? Do they expect a reason for overtime work or for the postponement of a vacation? And most of all, do they expect individual consideration or a sardines-in-the-can approach?

Discover these expectations, and you've opened up a whole new world of understanding yourself. From the sardonic "What's in it for me?" to the platonic "Where do I really fit in here?" a supervisor should know that his actions will provide part of an answer to these management and employee questions. Employees will always see themselves and weigh their worth by the way a supervisor treats them. If he's too busy to take time to listen, the employee feels left out. If he takes time and is too short and curt, the employee feels personally disliked. If the supervisor delivers ultimatums, the employee feels, "He wants to get rid of me." Each supervisory move results in counter management-employee moves, and without a knowledge of these expectations the understanding of yourself in relation to your job will be negligible, and the lack of it usually is harmful.

Harold J. Leavitt said that "the manager is his own best management mechanism." The manager who first studies himself will create a good base from which to build up to the characteristics of the people he manages. What, then, can you see in yourself as supervisor or manager which has common ground with the people around you?

1. You will see things differently than other people;

in fact, your needs may be another man's poison. Even the so-called "truth" may be untrue to another person. Differences in perception cannot be ignored; they are the main determinants of behavior.

2. When you encounter frustration, it's because you feel you can't overcome an obstacle and your well-being is in danger. When you meet this obstacle, aggression takes place. If your confidence is high, your aggression goes at the obstacle; if your confidence in yourself is low, your aggression will be directed toward yourself. You will "sense" this frustration when you can't get to your goal.

3. Your personality, like all others, is geared to meet most conflicting needs which will force you to make decisions in one direction or another. When the decision seems impossible, the resulting reaction could be catastrophic. Your need, drive, tension, desire, want, or motive (call it whatever you wish) *goes somewhere for some reason.* Your behavior is *caused, motivated, and goal-directed.* Understanding these things about yourself will help you to understand other people.

It was Harry Emerson Fosdick who said that "Life consists not simply in what heredity and environment do to us but in what we make out of what they do to us." Problems, like money in the bank, will compound themselves. Some supervisors compound their fears; others seek friction and continue to make more serious mistakes than their previous ones; still others can't get

through the day without walking the tightrope of frustration. Ask yourself these questions. Answer them as honestly as you can. You may find you're on the road of
better understanding yourself. Haven't you heard often
that the recognition and understanding of a problem
is half its solution?

| *Am I—* | *Where, When, and Why?* |
|---|---|
| The knot knitter? | When am I most likely to get tied up in knots? What causes me to worry more than anything else? Do I understand everything I fear? |
| The fact fighter? | Do I have a realistic point of view toward my job and my employees? Do I deal constructively with on-the-job problems? Am I willing to compromise when I have the facts? |
| The friction finder? | Must I always have my own way? Can I stand interruptions, or do they upset me? Am I a routine hound who becomes irritable over small disruptions? |
| The mistake maker? | What are the biggest mistakes I make on the job? Do I analyze these mistakes, or am I always making excuses |

*Am I—*

for them? Do I repeat the same mistakes or try to learn from experience?

The frustration feeder?

What causes me to "blow my top" more than anything else? When some things go wrong, am I cool, calm, and collected? Why don't my employees do exactly what I tell them to do?

The selfish supervisor?

Do I insist on all the credit for the work my employees do? Do I take time to pat people on the back when they deserve it? Do I understand and practice the golden rule?

The abnormal adjuster?

Do my employees think I'm cooperative and flexible? What makes me unable to adjust to new situations? What steps can I take to adjust myself to doing a better job as supervisor?

The headache hustler?

Do I get sick too often? If I do, when am I apt to feel worse? Is it when things go wrong?

| *Am I—* | *Where, When, and Why?* |
|---|---|
| The chronic complainer? | What is my biggest complaint? Do I complain too much about some of or all my employees? What are my complaints about myself? |

You can't answer these questions by looking at your shadow. It will require a hard, long look at your substantial self!

# SELECTION AND PLACEMENT

### crystal gazing or sound judgment?

Human resources are your most important assets. Without them, there would be no movement or progress in your job, your company, and your country. Human resources are fluid, flexible, forceful, and fast-changing. They add up to more than 2,000,800,000 man- and woman-hours *weekly* in American business and industry; some of it moves from Maine to California, from unskilled to skilled, from basement to board room. Your company has basic similarities with hundreds of other organizations across the nation: Some of your stockholders may own a part of other businesses, or the company may use the same type of machinery as another to get its work done, bend steel, and pour concrete to expand into new buildings, sell to mutual customers, expand together in neighboring territories, and draw upon the same labor markets for manpower. But perhaps the payroll clerk, pipe fitter, or purchasing agent in your company acts differently from the way he acts in another company. His ability to produce, his willingness to cooperate, and his desire to stay on the job can mean a lively, stimulating, and healthy existence for you and your company.

The art of managing this manpower, without question, belongs to the supervisor. To begin with, this manpower doesn't knock on any door. It is first discovered, then selected; it is placed and then developed. By whom? By you, its supervisor. The investment in dollars and cents for each of your employees is a big one. The stenographer, initially employed at $3,600 a year, at the completion of twenty-five years of service as private secretary to the president at $7,200 a year has cost more than $150,000 in salary payments alone and more than likely another $30,000 in employee benefits. A total investment in dollars for a college graduate with technical training with similar length of service may well stagger to a tumescent $2,000,000. Is it any wonder that most companies realize that from the crop of young men and women they select today will come tomorrow's harvest of foremen, supervisors, managers, directors, and presidents? Glance over your company's organization chart. How many of your top-ranking men started as junior sales trainees, junior engineers, mail clerks, accounting clerks? Probably quite a few. As job seekers they felt they were making "the most important decision of my life" as they faced the employment interview. Doesn't the job seeker feel he is throwing his entire background and experience into a company? Isn't it a gamble which he hopes will net for him and his dependents a satisfying and rewarding life—intellectually, socially, and economically?

Keen selection is as important to the new employee as it is to you and your company. The introduction of the right people into the organization is a vital managerial responsibility, a function of the supervisor's job, in spite of helpful screening efforts by personnel men or by friends of friends. In getting the right man for the right job, three considerations should be made:

1. Will this man "fit in"?
2. How well can he do the job?
3. How well will he do the job?

No penny-in-the-slot machine will produce a card with the answers. Each job seeker has his own coin. As he sits across your desk, you will begin to evaluate how well he will fit in by learning about his relationships with other people and what he thinks of himself. You will discover how well he can do the job by his previous work experience, his education and training, his special skills and aptitudes. With careful and skillful probing questions, his whole world of motivation will open up, enabling you to consider his willingness to do the job.

Several years ago the National Industrial Conference Board reported that 30 million job changes a year cost industry approximately 10 billion dollars annually.* Other studies have revealed that some of this waste could have been avoided if greater care had been taken in the employee-selection process. The Conference Board, reporting on 501 companies, also found that all of them look carefully at the man before putting him on the payroll. This included not only applicants for salaried jobs but all applicants for jobs paid by the hour. It was true for the lowest-paid laborer to the highest-paid executive.

Forecasting is a widely used activity in management circles. It is applied to projected Christmas sales, next year's steel prices, the number of unemployed construction workers, competitive production quotas, and the new skirt length this coming spring. Because of it, improved planning and production plans can be set. Forecasting about people has not been as easy; in fact, we can be rather sure that each day someone is failing rather miserably in predicting how a certain employee will fare in a certain job. To help improve this prediction, profes-

---

* *Management Record*, vol. 21, nos. 7–8, p. 228, National Industrial Conference Board, Inc., New York, July-August, 1959.

sional and popular journals are crammed full these days with tales of research, experience, and judgments about interviewing techniques, personality tests, interview rating forms, reference-checking procedures, and the necessary qualifying traits essential to success in an American business. Not all of this mass of information gives "the pat answer" to selection problems, although some business and industrial people now find it easier to say more than "The applicant looks all right," "I don't know too much about him, but we'd better give him a chance," or "How am I to know?" when the boss asks, "Say, Joe, what did you think of that guy?" Facing every supervisor or manager, every vice president or president, is the requirement that he evaluate an available somebody against an available job. Among the selection techniques available to you in making this evaluation is the interview. "Looking the man over" in an interview can go a long way in helping build a work force; it can tell how this man will fit in and whether he will do the job and how well. Let's now look over some of the steps in this evaluation process in which a potential employee and you are the central players in a scene called the *interview*.

### The interview, generally speaking

Paul W. Boynton of Socony-Vacuum Oil Company said that "The interview is a free exchange of information, based on good will, and predicated on a desire to find the person best suited for a particular job." His statement is interesting in light of the fact that so many think of the employment interview only as a chance to get information from the job seeker. Boynton's words are focused on a more meaningful and larger screen. In addition to getting information from the job seeker, the interviewer should also see to it that the job seeker gets enough information about the job and the company to help *him* decide if he is the right man for the right job. A review of the current job description and job specification for the particular job opening will give the interviewee specifics about the content of the job. It may prevent that ugly moment on a second day of work when a new employee says with regret, "Gee, Mr. Stender, you never really told me what was in this job. I just don't think I'll be able to handle it." Or worse, perhaps on a third morning, the case of the "no show" and your hours of reflection about "What did I do wrong this time?"

The interviewer is like the salesman: He, too, has a product to sell, a given job in a given company. Many job seekers will walk over to another firm because the interviewer lacked enthusiasm and failed to point out why the job is a good one, the company a good place to work. The supervisor and the company, integral parts of the community in which they exist, add to better or poorer public relations as a result of the hundreds of interviews they conduct in a career lifetime. When word gets around that your place is a good place to work, recruitment efforts are not as strenuous. Understanding the interview process includes realizing that the process is a tense, foreboding, and ill-at-ease experience for many applicants. Your desire to find the best person should be strong enough to make you take steps to soften the interviewing atmosphere by creating a friendly situation in which talking and exchanging information will come easily. A good-will exchange of information, a desire for the right man for the right job, intelligent salesmanship, and a sense of public relations and careful evaluation and interpretation of the facts you've gathered are all part of the process in accomplishing a complete and successful interview.

### The other foot

People being interviewed for a job know that their responses may or may not get them the job. Because of this, most interviewees will put their best foot forward. If the interviewer asks, "How did you like your previous jobs?" the answer is usually, "Swell. I really liked all my three jobs." But perhaps two months ago, while still employed in his last job, the interviewee was at his doctor's office, paying $10 for professional advice about a troublesome stomach and telling the doctor that it wasn't just not liking the work he was doing, but that he just couldn't take the perpetual pressure from his boss.

People do play differently to different audiences. It's

up to the interviewer to see that his questions are so phrased that the interviewee does not always come out with the answer he thinks is expected. Instead of asking, "How did you like your previous jobs?" he might ask, "Which job did you like best and why?" Answers to such questions may still be guesses about the expected answer, but they do give a truer picture of the applicant sitting across your desk. There is little doubt among interview experts about the value of what is termed the *nondirective* interview. The principle applied here makes a lot of common sense. The interviewer's questions are relatively open, with plenty of room for the interviewee to project into the interview his own feelings, his own likes and dislikes, his better or poorer attitudes. In using the nondirective method, if the interviewer feels he requires more specific information about the applicant, he can ask more direct questions to find out what he needs to know and then start the open process over again, with broad sweeping questions narrowing to hairline questions, if he feels it necessary to do so.

### Mirror, mirror, on the wall

Sigmund Freud is the first to have been credited with the idea that the products of a person's free associations are related to his inner drives and conflicts. An interviewer who allows his own free associations to run away with him can cause harm in the interviewing procedure.

In doing this, the interviewer is inclined to evaluate job seekers against himself and to reject potential employees who "differ" from his own personal standard. Who knows what underlying association the interviewer may have had with the rejected applicant who had red hair, too much space between his eyes, or a European-styled suit? It would be of no advantage to an organization if all its employees had brown hair and blue eyes, were 5 feet 8 inches tall, wore double-breasted suits and gray over-coats, and admired Arthur Godfrey. Uniformity, a second cousin of mediocrity, can cause a department or a company to be dull, unstimulating, and stagnant. Different but complementary personalities, a variety of skills and talents, distinct and thought-provoking points of view can produce more vital group and departmental relationships.

### Count the blessings

A knowledge of what it takes to do the job that the applicant is being considered for cannot be overemphasized. This is important because it concerns the traits, the qualities, and the skills you are hoping to find in the applicant. Often, a candidate has all the basic qualifications, but the interviewer rejects the candidate, perhaps after only a few minutes of the interview have elapsed. Why? Because the candidate revealed a weakness. This can easily happen. Many interviewers are more on the alert for weaknesses than they are for strengths, even though such weaknesses may have nothing to do with whether or not the candidate may be able to perform the duties of the job. Lots of good men are lost in this way. Many "average employees" are hired in this way. If we accept the fact that everyone has some faults, in varying degrees, then the man we hire has faults. But he also may have some outstanding strengths. Being on the alert for strengths, and not for individual weaknesses, *in view of the job demands* will fortify the interviewing process. Of course, there's not much point in developing an interview with a truck driver who has a poor accident record, with an accounting clerk who can't add, or with a well driller who doesn't like outside work. Look for strong points first, place weak points in proper perspective, evaluate both in terms of the demands of the job.

### All that glitters is not gold

An applicant, early in the interview, may tell the interviewer that he is paying for his younger brother's education. The interviewer, just four short years ago, may have paid for his younger brother's college education also. With this in common, the interviewer feels "warm inside" and wants to take a longer, deeper look into this applicant's history. It's easy for him to agree with everything that's said. The applicant's work experience, family background, education, mental alertness all seem to be exactly what the interviewer is looking for. Is it possible that subjectively this interviewer built a cozy wall around this interviewing situation? This "halo effect" is defined as giving an applicant an over-all rating based on a single factor.

The over-all rating may be a positive or a negative one. What would happen if the shoe were on the other foot? Let's assume that the interviewer had paid for 3½ years of a college education for a younger brother who never made the grade and that such an experience had been distasteful to him. Might he have rated the applicant negative all the way down the line? Beware of isolated likes and dislikes which may come across the room in the form of soft blue eyes, the Roman nose, president of the senior class, bushy eyebrows, tight lips, or a heavily starched white collar. Some successful salesmen have Roman noses, some executive vice presidents have bushy eyebrows, and many job floaters have soft blue eyes.

### Testing: the psychological frank

It is obvious in our country that the psychological test is as popular as the hot dog. Almost any job applicant today can claim having taken a bite of this seemingly here-to-stay phenomenon. Although originally developed for use by schools and clinics, going businesses and going-out-of-business firms have wasted no time in latching on to tests and their score keys. Harry Levinson, director of the Division of Industrial Mental Health at the Menninger Foundation, discussed the shortcomings of the personality test in industrial situations in an address be-

fore the American Psychological Association. Authorita-
tively, he asserted that "Failure to reach policies more
sound than those which are presently being employed
will bring down upon the heads of psychologists the same
appellations which for a long time were thrown at industrial physicians who, because they were regarded as
company spies, became anathema to employees."

With the moving of the personality test from the psychologist's office to the personnel office, certain safeguards
have disappeared regarding its use, administration, and
interpretation. Some consultants today even claim to be
able to transmit the mystic power of personality interpretation to the unschooled psychological mind in less
than a month's time, and they claim that in this way *le
champagne* can be separated from *le vin ordinaire*. Applicants who were brought up on the principle of blood,
sweat, and tears are now hurried into isolation booths
for three, four, and more hours of tests. Test questions
investigate their motivations, search their inspirations,
and delve into their sex relations. The answers which
roll off the reproducers, sorters, and calculators are not
always the hidden motives, drives, or attitudes familiar
to the applicant, much less those which he or she wants
to hear. In particular, the "turn-downs" have been the
most skeptical and dubious about the value of these tests.

Amidst the furor, learned psychologists and psychom-
etricians, in and out of industry, have come to some
sound conclusions. Boiled down to as few words as pos-

sible, their consensus runs something like this: Research has made significant strides in learning about personality traits in the fields of selection, placement, and job satisfaction. Not all of this knowledge is in the form of a test which can easily be used by business and industry.

This means that many of the personality tests available on the market today may have been *borrowed* by the personnel office from the psychology lab or clinic where the patient, or employee, if you will, is under a completely different set of circumstances. There, in fact, are many pickets in the growing wall of opposition to test. One well-known spokesman, William H. Whyte, Jr., has proposed that tests are not congruous with the American ideal of individual freedom. He goes as far as to question whether or not the "hidden" self is any of the boss's business. Saul W. Gellerman, psychological consultant, has written,*

> What kind of information does management need about an individual's personality to make sensible hiring, placement and training decisions? It seems obvious that superfluous probing, which neither improves management's decision-making nor contributes to the testee's welfare, should be done away with. Being a personnel man or even a psychologist does not confer the license to poke about in somebody else's private affairs—unless one has his consent and can demonstrate that it will be helpful to him. Tests should be used

* "The Ethics of Personality Testing," *Personnel*, AMA, New York, November-December, 1958.

only to obtain data that are directly relevant to the probable work performance of the testee, or that will help management in developing him. . . . Some deviations, of course, are very much management's business. Alcoholism, psychopathic tendencies, and other conditions which affect reliability, should be interpreted (not just reported) to management.

What, then, is your role in this controversial area? If tests results are available, you should realize that

1. Tests are probably here to stay

2. Many tests can be of real value in the selection and placement of human resources

3. Test results should be only *one* of the determining factors in making decisions

4. Generally, varieties other than personality tests are more meaningful in industrial situations

5. Test information is a "private affair"

### Putting the pieces together

A lot of information can be gathered in a twenty- or thirty-minute interview. Since the man with whom you've just talked is to be accepted or rejected as a member of your work force, the decision is yours. Seldom will it be an all-black or all-white decision. Will this man succeed in the job which you have in mind? It's a good job: assistant business promotion manager. Of the three candidates you interviewed, Jack Tulley sticks in your mind. Bill Tower runs a close second but didn't quite succeed in one of his previous jobs. If only there weren't so many ifs and buts. Supposing Bill had had a different boss, what if he had been given that long-sought-after assistant, what about that budget cut, was it easy for Bill to work with a different sales manager each six months, and what would have happened if the ad agency treated the business promotion department with kid gloves as much as it did the sales office? Might Bill have been more successful? Was Bill's personality solely responsible for the so-called failure, or did the situation account for any of this? Plenty of gray area, isn't there? An over-all decision has to be made. You will now have to weigh the man against the job as a whole and conclude whether he is qualified or not. At this point, your efforts culminate. Here's what should happen.

*Weigh what you heard:*

What the applicant told you about his successes and salary demands, his experience and expectations, his flexibility and failures should be weighed.

Bill Tower said he was getting no place fast over at Consolidated Transport, Inc. What did he mean? Did he mean jobwise, salarywise? Did he mean happy hours at work or just no time for the wife and kids? If he meant there was no chance for promotion, exactly where did he think he belonged on the organization chart? If it was salary, what did he think he was worth? What would it take to make him happy, forty or sixty hours a week? How deep-rooted is his need to leave the office at five on the dot every night in order not to upset the routine at home, annoy the wife, and miss kissing the kids goodnight? When you feel you know why he was getting no place fast, translate it to your own department. Is what threatened Bill's success in his last job present in this one?

Jack Tulley said he "got along real well with everyone." As far as you could tell, there were no fuzzy areas about Jack and the boss. Jack's job was mostly working with and through people. He was on the last job for almost five years and had spent six years in the job before that. Almost everything Jack said was people-oriented. He had good things to say about people he had worked with. He talked about an old school teacher he had admired all these years. And what about that war buddy of his who is now employed in our Chicago office? What did he have to say about Jack?

*Test the tale:*

After the interview, there are several things you can do to verify what the applicant told you during the interview.

Bill Tower confused dates at least three times during the interview. Many people can't remember

dates, but Bill's hesitations and confusion reached
the point where the subject was finally dropped.
Later, a check against his application form did not
corroborate what he had corrected during the interview.

It was easy the next morning when talking to the
Chicago office to ask to speak to Jack's friend. Jack
was right. They had known each other in the Pacific.
They had traveled together from Hawaii to Guam
to Wake. Reference letters were sent to previous
employers. One firm said Bill Tower had never
been employed by them. Another firm reported
that Jack Tulley was above average on all counts.
A letter from Jack's college authorities said he was
voted the most popular man on the campus in his
junior year. Of course, reference checks are not always as reliable as one would like, but in this case
they were at least another step in validating impres-
sions gained by the interviewer and information
given by the candidates.

*Weigh the man against the job:*

The minimum traits or qualifications needed for satisfactory performance should be kept in mind. To what
extent does the applicant meet these qualifications? To
answer this as thoroughly as is possible, some evaluation
techniques other than the interview and reference checks
will have to be considered. These include the results of

a physical examination and psychological-test results. Although in varying degrees, physical exertion is a part of working and living. It is important to know what physical limitations the applicant may have. From across the desk, it is almost impossible to find out about poor vision, a heart ailment, tuberculosis, or a hernia. These impairments show up as a result of a physical examination; finding one of them does not usually rule out an applicant, but it does suggest and often determine where the applicant can do his best work.

Jack Tulley passed his physical examination. There were some question-mark areas about his test results, however. The test report in part read as follows: "Mr. Tulley has above-average intelligence. Problem situations do not throw him. As a rule, he does not become emotionally involved in work problems. As the job is the most important thing in his mind, he believes that all else, for himself and others, should take on a secondary significance. Because of this attitude, he can, on occasion, be highly critical of those who work for him. He asks as much of his subordinates as he does of himself...."

A discussion with the testing or placement section allayed some of the fears of Tulley's "being highly critical of others...." A complete review of test results in light of the information from the interview and reference checks and emphasis on

Tulley's strengths rather than his seeming weakness clarified what negative aspects there were in the report.

*Now make the decision:*

Weighing the individual against the job, analyzing the full information gathered from the individual during the interview, how objectively the findings were appraised, and your knowledge and understanding of people and jobs should clearly tell you to say one of two things: "I'd better take a look at someone else," or "I shall hire this man."

# 5

# TRAINING

## appetizer or full meal?

What the famous Samuel Johnson said in the late eighteenth century about Scottish learning could well apply in the mid-twentieth century to American industrial training: "Their learning is like bread in a besieged town: every man gets a little but no man gets a full meal."

In the American frame of reference, the concept of the self-made man sits high on our industrial pedestal. A closer look, however, at some of our homemade heroes will show that somewhere along the way a full meal administered in their training diets may be responsible for part of the success they and their companies enjoy. Though individual success is synonymous with individual effort, one of the greatest satisfactions to any leader of people will be the unobtrusive and often screened fact that you helped push him up the ladder.

If you take a minute to review your job description, somewhere you will see these words: "Responsible for the training and development of employees." No doubt, your management has emphasized training and personnel development from time to time. Perhaps, at this time, you may be getting weary waiting for someone up the line to carry a neat little training package on a silver platter down the line to you. You ask again and again, "When is someone going to do something about it?" The awful truth is that they may be waiting for *you* to do something about it. Passing the buck in the area of training responsibility is a common practice. You can hear these expressions in any plant, office, or shop: "Stick around and watch that guy for a week or so. . . . I thought they taught you that at college. . . . You sure wasted a full week at the company training school."

Teaching and learning can be the most vexing activities in one's experience. In 350 B.C., it wasn't easy for Plato to teach Aristotle. Centuries later, Samuel Butler cried, "Learning, that cobweb of the brain, profane, erroneous and vain." And not too long ago, in the late nineteenth century, the idea of a trained employee was blocked by an economic frontier. Training budget? Bah! Humbug! Besides, it was an era when with little or no education, little or no cultural background, men could and did build fortunes. Those turn-of-the-century magnates, since passed away, never dreamed that the industrial dynasties they created would live on, much less undergo undreamed-of expansion, undreamed-of problems.

Before World War I, supervisors and managers who had learned everything they knew the hard way wanted the new employee to go through the same grueling process. What, give away my trade secrets? During the war years, to increase our productive capacity to limitless heights, employers started to sing a different training tune. Minors and Aunt Minnie, Grandma, and young Gertie knew little about the jobs for which they were hired, but employers were amazed at what could happen to these novices, and to production quotas, with a little planned training. Though they failed to meet job specifications at employment time, these new employees could top quotas if they were shown what to do and how to do it. Employers began to like this training tune. Whatever else your job may be said to be, there is no question that a great deal of it must be concerned with teaching. A little mental checking will tell you that on some days, almost half your time is given to teaching while someone is learning. When was the last time you found a nice shiny red apple on your desk?

We have heard much about the readiness of the

learner; the question before us now is, "What about the readiness of the teacher?" It has been said, and with some truth, that the average supervisor or manager is poorly prepared for this part of his job. True, he knows his subject, but does he have the ability to communicate it? He may have an abundance of paternal patience, but will he take the time to do a thorough training job? He may be aware of numerous errors in his bailiwick, but how brightly burns his flaming desire to teach? There are three basic and general reasons why the training function in your job is as important as everyone says it is:

1. A shortage of manpower threatens you.
2. Untrained employees create problem situations.
3. Employees must learn in order to develop.

### Manpower shortage

Louis Ruthenburg, in discussing a growing crisis in apprentice training, said: *

> There seems to be a smug assumption going the rounds that automation, electronic data processing and other manifestations of technological progress are eliminating the need for the skilled craftsman. Nothing could be further from the truth. The skilled worker has always been the pivot on which every industrial operation turns, and advancing technology, far from reducing the need for his services, actually increases [it]. . . . Yet, today, this group—upon whom, to a large

* "The Crisis in Apprentice Training," *Personnel*, AMA, New York, July-August, 1959.

degree, our industrial future depends—is shrinking at an alarming rate. Its older members are dying off and not nearly enough young men are being trained to replace them. If American industry does not take steps to reverse this trend, its impact upon our entire social, political and economic structure will be little short of disastrous.

Many voices similar to Ruthenburg's have cried that the long-range threat to the American economy is not necessarily a shortage of jobs or work but simply a shortage of skilled employees. Economic forecasts of American growth are glowing. Since the last war, they say, jobs have been plentiful, expansion limitless, and research sky-high, and the most reliable pollsters predict more jobs, newer products, and strange new industries. But what about the labor force? Who's going to do the work? In *America's Next Twenty Years* * Peter Drucker tells us that "The major events that determine the future have already happened—irrevocably.... Everyone who will join the workforce within the next eighteen or twenty years has by now been born.... The economic population of the next twenty years (its numbers, age and sex distribution) is not just predictable; *it is already in being.*" Charles A. Myers † warns of a serious

* Peter Drucker, *America's Next Twenty Years*, Harper & Bros., New York, 1957.

† Director, Industrial Relations Sections, M.I.T. From "Manpower Management, the Challenge of the 1960s," *Supervisory Management*, AMA, November, 1959.

shortage of male employees between the ages of twenty-five and forty-five in the foreseeable future. He says, "This is no wild guess; it is based on the number of people in those future age groups who have already been born. For example, in 1965, there will actually be 700,000 fewer men aged 25–35 than there were in 1955."

You may wonder what these predictions mean to you. If these expected shortages become real, more than ever you will have to give special attention to training, developing, and retaining your employees. The problem reduces itself to a matter of practicality. Your younger employees today will be your skilled employees tomorrow. They will become assistant supervisors, senior technicians, and not-much-older executives. If these expected shortages become real, and there is sound reason to believe they will, you will have to place greater emphasis not only on improved selection and placement techniques but on more improved training methods, as well. If your work is to get out, there can be no shortage of skilled help in your ranks. To prevent numerous job openings in your department, the well-trained permanent employee must be one of your perpetual objectives.

### The bowling pins of the training alley

From where you stand, take a good long look down your work alley. How many problem situations do you recognize? You'll recognize at least one of the following problem situations where training is a must. A training "strike" would mean a complete upset of the following pins. How well do you score?

PIN 1: *The newcomer or transferred employee*

No matter how much previous experience, education, or training a new employee may have had, he has come face-to-face with a new environment, a new set of circumstances, new work methods, and a new boss. Is this new employee so competent that he is able to step into his new situation without some training?

PIN 2: *The new assignment*

In every organization, assignments will vary. You may not have known it last evening, but this morning your department and your people have a new task to perform. Who will do it and how is your problem. The training methods to be used to accomplish the objective will be set by you. The formulation of training plans assures that new jobs appearing on the scene will get done and done well.

PIN 3: *The overflowing scrap bucket*

A constant eye on the scrap can may serve as a way of measuring satisfactory work performance, crude though the measurement may be. When the rejects pile up, investigation of training needs may give the clue to determining how to go about improving individual job performance. This should be an easy pin to bowl over.

### PIN 4: *The alley wrecker*

The employee who spoils goods may also spoil himself (and other employees) with careless accidents on the job. A count of the sore thumbs, twisted fingers, and broken toes should serve as a reminder that training has not been fully accomplished. When an accident occurs in your work area (and the employee has been cared for), take a look at the facts of the accident case and determine whether additional training may have prevented the mishap.

### PIN 5: *Overtime of the undertrained*

Whether it be noticed by personal observation or by studying individual overtime records, excess overtime may not always be linked to a legitimate load of work. One possible explanation may be that overtime hours are the direct result of a lack of knowledge regarding one's job. Not knowing how to do his work during regular work hours may keep an undertrained individual on overtime until he feels he has the problem licked. Proper training in the first place will save many costly overtime hours of pay and deadly overtime hours of fatigue.

PIN 6: *Turnover of the untrained*

Is there any question that job dissatisfaction is a prime reason for leaving a job? Is there any question that job satisfaction implies job know-how? Is there any question that job know-how means adequate training? The frustrations created in the individual who doesn't know what he is doing are many and inevitably lead to dissatisfaction and finally to resignation (or dismissal by the superior who is not training-minded). The careful recruitment, selection, and placement of the right man for the right job may be all in vain when training time and attention have been bypassed. This headache situation multiplied can only end in migraine. If the loss of would-be good employees plagues you, analyze the amount, the caliber, and the conscientious training attention you gave. Generally, trained employees don't turn over.

PIN 7: *The untrained complainer*

Complaints, gripes, and chips on the shoulder are all part of a normal workday. All of us take these things for granted until we get fed up with a dose of really chronic complaints. This chronic condition is often identified early in the game; usually, the chronic complainer is an employee who is not quite sure how to handle his part of the job. Perhaps, in self-defense, he commences to grind out the complaints, many of which take their

toll on his innocent and trained co-workers. It's time
again for an evaluation of a training situation. If the
chronic complaints cease after additional training aid
has been applied, score this one up to training time.

PIN 8: *The bulbous bottleneck*

The bulge in the production belt snaps it in two.
Anxieties are rampant and nerves are red-hot. The boss
is ready to fire someone and the employee is ready to
quit. How did this ever happen? Why are we stuck? This
situation is almost always traceable to the poor human
being who has been around long enough to know but
for some reason or another didn't really know better.
His unskilled hands, his untrained mind, and his un-
taught manner is the pivot of the problem. Bottlenecks
and the resultant chaos caused by a malfunctioning employee require prompt training attention. Better take
him off the production belt; put him back on after careful training has been administered. Before he stretches
his next bottleneck, the wise manager will carefully review the situation to see if it requires training.

PIN 9: *Training the hard-to-obtain*

Each year, decade, and generation seem to have one
or more classifications of workers who are in demand,
be they secretaries or servicemen, turret-lathe or tab
operators. Many companies, after the last war, could fill
each job opening only after planned training programs

had been applied to present personnel. Shortages of various kinds still persist in our labor markets. Training hard-to-obtain personnel in your environment is a must if these sought-after people are to be employed and are to remain with you in a productive and efficient relationship.

PIN 10: *Training because of human nature*

Each human being is subject to new experiences, new ideas, and different contacts as he lives his life, and each sphere into which we are drawn changes us to some degree, however slight. Month by month or year by year, we are never quite the same. The changes may seem imperceptible or even appear as though they are not taking place. Nevertheless, they do occur. Just as a child's height periodically measured with a yardstick shows increases that were daily imperceptible to the parent's eye, managers are asked to rate a subordinate at specified times, in order to record changes in behavior; it is not always easy to recognize these changes in people with whom we work daily. Don't we mentally make note of the graying hair or additional 10 pounds of obesity of an old friend whom we have not seen for a few years? Changes are not always for the good, and the employee who last year made significant strides beyond mediocre performance may have slipped back into the doldrums of dull do-nothingness. Here again, human nature, being what it is, may necessitate another retraining situation for you if the usual heart-to-heart chat has garnered no results. Carelessness, indifference, and apathy are not unusual temporary detours for the proficient employee. When you recognize them as such, there's your chance to take steps to help that employee get back on the right road.

### Learning—a lifelong process

The greatest mistake anyone can make is to suppose that knowledge can be acquired by passing through high school or college. As the diploma is handed to the young graduate, he can be pardoned the illusions that he has "completed his education." It is only a matter of months before this young adult realizes how little he knows and how much there is still to learn. His formal schooling, a drop in the bucket of education, opens his eyes to the big, big world outside the high school building or college campus. What he learns later in life opens them wider.

### Monkeys aren't always "the craziest people"

Psychology tells us that learning takes place at nervous-system crossroads between the incoming and outgoing nerve currents, that cerebral activity leads and guides the learning process. Animals and men learn in this same way. We can trace early animal learning experiments back to Greece when Aristotle was a youthful biologist. A museum in a training zoo might display these experimental and historical signs:

Goldfish can learn to tell the difference between dim, medium, and bright lights.

Earthworms can learn to work their way out of T mazes.

Chicks can quickly learn by trial and error to find food in a Thorndike maze.

Cats can learn to find their way to a goal by operating a mechanism that will make it available.

A dog can release itself from a cage by operating a simple mechanism.

Hungry rats can go off on a learning spree; the satisfied ones will stay home.

Apes can learn by observing other apes.

Apes inside a cage can learn to reach food with a pole if the pole is placed between the food and the ape.

One smart ape, Sultan, piled four boxes one on top of the other to get food hanging from the top of his cage. He also connected two sticks to reach for food.

Monkeys can learn to use the right key to raid an icebox.

Hundreds of experiments in animal learning clearly show that better coordination is achieved, few errors are made, and learning time is shortened when the animal is given an opportunity to repeat a series of somewhat similar responses to a somewhat similar series of stimuli patterns, *when there is a goal in sight.*

### What makes Johnny learn?

Experiments in infant learning show that although each child has his own individual rate of growth, infants learn rapidly during the first two years of life. Behavioral changes are made most rapidly, and the basic growth pattern is almost the same for each child. Continual practice is the root of most learning in young children. As they grow up, desires are formed, skills are developed, ideas come to mind, and they express likes and dislikes. Soon, with more and more practice, habits are formed. Imagine the number of things a child must learn in a few short years: to tell time, to be prompt, to hang up his coat, to make the bed, play the piano, tell the truth, shut up, read the book, get up, ride the bike, be neat, live like Abe, be brave, and tie his shoelace. Child experts disclaim that children learn one thing at a time. Instead, they say, Johnny is learning a multitude of other things while learning to keep his balance on two wheels. True, it may not be intentional, but it happens anyway. On the bike, he learns to judge distance, stop short, talk to others, name streets, and identify faces in the crowd.

What Johnny learns is directly proportionate to the comfortable and good feeling he gets from it. And this seems to go with him throughout his life. As a young pilot trainee, Johnny is not comfortable with his flight instructor. He derives little pleasure and no satisfaction from his hours at the controls. His grades in the air are hardly passable. Yet, on check-out flights, the check-out pilot instructor and Johnny derive mutual satisfaction, and Johnny's grades approach 100.

Johnny learns better by a constant repetition of the thing learned. Think of those early piano lessons, for example, or of learning Shakespeare's "To be, or not to be: that is the question: ..."

### Human versus animal learning

Briefly, what are the significant differences between animal and human learning? In spite of the fact that your terrier Skippy will sit down when told to do so, verbal communication with animals is impossible, whereas human beings can talk with their fellow human beings and tell each other what they feel, remember, and experience. Man's brain is better developed, and therefore he can work better mentally; he can compose ideas about outer space and time. As he is a more complex entity, he confronts more complex problems and situations, attacking more, solving more. Man is a superior observer, a more refined manipulator. Why, then, do we bother about the goldfish? And the earthworm? Experiments with simple and more complex animal forms have given us considerable insight into the learning process. Experiments with infants, children, and adults have given us knowledge of the areas of human learning and behavior that form the basis of psychological and social science. Let's face these facts.

Employees cannot grow to full capacity in a work environment which stunts their growth, any more than polar fur-bearing animals can be raised in the Caribbean. The atmosphere of training and development can be created by the man in charge who realistically recognizes each employee as an individual, with different traits, needs, personalities, and learning capacities. In understanding the employee who is to be trained and developed, you will need to consider these fundamental concepts, all derived from the myriad of experimental missions, whether they were performed in the animal or human worlds.

### Training commences with the trainee as he is

You might think of a new employee, the trainee, as locked in an 8-foot-square cage with his physical and mental abilities. He is simply stuck with them and also with the circumstances of his life which these have brought him. What comes to him from outside the cage —how often he is fed and bathed—the number of people who come by and pet him on the back—the rules and regulations of the keeper—all are social codes of his world, and these will determine the direction, the scope, and the basis of his learning. The trainee, like most employees, wants to learn and train for immediate needs and not for those related to retirement years. The laborer who is a good trainee and who has keenly set his sights on the job general superintendent of a massive construction crew is exceptional. Most laborers will train easily if it is clear to them that they will reach their goal posts in six or twelve months, this year and not next.

### Training goals and excitement go hand in hand

If you were to chart the goals you have had in terms of five-year periods in your life, you probably would find different goals associated with each five-year period. It might be something like this:

First five years:  the bottle, the teddy bear, or mother's arms

Second five years:  peanut butter and jelly, a bat and ball, or a storybook

Third five years:  a bicycle, an hour later to bed, or the girl next door

Fourth five years:  another girl, the college of your choice, or that varsity letter

Fifth five years:  the right job in the right company, a salesman's award, or the next merit increase

Tenth five years:  that vice-presidential job, a new house, or an air trip to Europe

Training and excitement go hand in hand, because excitement in its own special way helps us to remember certain turns along the way to our goals. The goals change because in life there seems to be an endless number of new and stimulating situations. What you found exciting about the bat and ball years ago would not cause you to exert the same energies thirty years later that you summon up for that new and better-paying job. Have not the price tags changed on all your goals as the years have gone by? If as trainer you recognize the trainee's world of interest and excite him along these lines, the chore of training will be facilitated.

### Training means knowing how you're doing

When people say we learn by experience, they also mean that we learn by recognition of our mistakes. Unless the trainer takes time out to chart the progress of his trainee, the trainee can keep on making the same mistake over and over again. In any training situation, knowing how he's doing motivates the trainee and speeds the training process. And this can go beyond the number of key punches per minute, the number of eggs sorted in two minutes, or the number of square feet painted in three minutes. It is common to see accident-free mile records of twenty different departments on the company's bulletin board or a list of educational courses completed by employees in a company magazine article. This is one way of allowing people to know how they're doing. Check yourself the next time you're training one of your kids to swim: "Thata boy, Jimmy, watch it now, kick your legs a little harder—

keep them a little more straight—use both arms—you're splashing too much—watch your breathing—a mouthful of water isn't going to kill you—thata boy, Jimmy, you're doing fine."

### Training means encouraging the better employees too

If all the time, patience, and devotion in the world were given to the poorer student, the below-average employee, or the antisocial teen-ager, the wheels of progress would turn slowly or perhaps not at all. No one should seriously question the advisability of having a home-relief office or the city's youth board, but one may ponder about the amount of time given to the mental have-nots in contrast to the haves. Duller students and the less bright employees usually work more nearly to their capacities than do the brighter students or the more intelligent employees. The satisfaction of reaching one's goal, the anticipation of a coveted reward, or possibly the fear of distasteful punishment will usually act as significant incentives or drives to learning by the brighter individuals, but similar drives and incentives usually do not cause any major upheaval in the productivity of the so-called have-nots. Training, then, goes along with emphasis on the trainable—the employee who clearly demonstrates a potential for absorbing what is offered. Too many of us take this better employee for granted, thinking it is enough to have him shift for himself, giving precious time to the guy who may get nowhere and losing one or more of the better employees. Words of encouragement to the bright high school senior by a thoughtful instructor may have been the decisive factor in sending that student on to greater explorations at the college level. This happens in the business and industrial world too.

### Training is coaching

An effective four-step job-instruction plan which was developed during World War II includes:

1. Prepare the employee
2. Present the job
3. Try out the employee
4. Follow through

Preparing an employee for a training situation means more than putting him at ease. Where new employees are concerned, there is some discomfort and nervousness in a new work situation. A sense of feeling comfortable and at home is necessary but the preparation should include much more than "Look Harry, this is all there is to do." In preparing the employee to learn, you should find out how much the trainee already knows about the task at hand. Without this knowledge on his part, going through repetitious tasks with the new employee will bore him. Arousing his interest is important too. Though at ease, the learner must feel that he is interested in learning. Talking to the trainee before the actual teaching process will reveal just about how much the trainee knows. This is a time saver also. Teaching the learner what he doesn't already know will also give a boost to his interest. Once the trainer knows how much the learner knows, once he recognizes the trainee's interest in the task to be learned and if he feels the trainee is at ease, only then can he go on to the next step.

You can only present a job after you have analyzed its inherent parts and know how they fit together. The trainee must be given one step at a time, with enough time to master each step. The trainer should tell him what is to be done and then show him how to do it. Of course, it is foolish to move on to the next learning phase until you are sure that the learner has learned part one before being exposed to part two, that he knows parts one and two before going on to part three and so forth. In individual training, you will see that employees differ in their learning time; in group situations this is more difficult to gauge but spot-check questions will help to see that everyone is up to par.

The third step calls for an employee tryout on what he has learned. The trainer stands by and watches the trainee go through each step of the task he has learned. If a mistake is made, the trainee should be given an opportunity to correct himself. The serious and competent trainer will know when he is satisfied with the learner's progress; you will know when the trainee is able to do the job.

Many trainers fall down on the fourth step: the follow-through. It may not sound important but it is. You can't end a training session with, "Okay Bud, you've got it down pat," and then walk away and forget the learner and what he has learned. Although the trainee may now be on his own, the trainer follows through by coming back every now and then to be sure that the correct procedure is being followed but—more important— he comes back to answer any questions the trainee may have. Follow-through solidifies the training process. With it, the trainee will develop into a well-trained employee and will require only a normal amount of supervision.

Skill and proficiency are developed by practice and repetition. What we have done best is usually what we have learned best. What we have learned best has generally been accompanied by some form of coaching or supervision. We remember considerably less of what we see and hear, somewhat more of what we say and do, but most of what we do when we are trimmed and pruned by the trainer. Alfred Bougeart put it this way: "The more an idea is developed, the more concise becomes its expression; the more a tree is pruned, the better is the fruit."

### What about you?

The Roman god Janus had two faces. One looked to the past and the other scanned the future. Like Janus, if you are to achieve success in your goal, turn your head backward to learn from experience, then turn it forward to understand and see how this learning will be applied to your hours on and off the job. It is part of your learning and training to see to it that your employees know what they are expected to do and how to do it. Unless you raise their job skills, the performance of individual employees and of the work team as a whole will remain static. The monotony of mediocrity will allow the process of disintegration to set in. Remember that your reputation as a leader depends on your reputation as a trainer. Remember the ways by which adults learn. Remember that four basic steps are involved in training: (1) establishing rapport with the trainee and seeing that he is ready to learn; (2) actually demonstrating what needs to be done and how; (3) seeing to it that the employee understands what needs to be done and how to do it; and (4) taking time to review the employee's progress as he is being trained, as he learns, as he is reviewed. Above all, keep repeating four famous lines written many years ago by Alexander Pope: *

A little learning is a dang'rous thing;
Drink deep, or taste not the Pierian spring;
There shallow draughts intoxicate the brain,
And drinking largely sobers us again.

* *An Essay on Criticism.*

# 6

# YOUR DELEGATION

### *silver-coated or clear glass?*

If we are to begin to understand the art of supervision, we'd better first define and clarify our termin-
ology to avoid the confusion inadvertently described by
Mrs. Malaprop in R. B. Sheridan's *The Rivals:* "If I
reprehend anything in this world, it is the use of my
oracular tongue, and a nice derangement of epitaphs."
*Authority, power,* and *leadership* are words commonly
used and confused; they are key words in this discussion.

Years ago Mary Parker Follett defined the first two, and her definitions are still valid. Authority, in our concept of democratic supervision, is "the formal right to require action of others." On the other hand, power is "the ability to make things happen." Aren't we all familiar with the prototype, in or out of our organizations, of the man with authority who simply can't make things happen? Today, after hundreds of years of studying a long history of organized human effort, most of us agree that authority is effective only when it is acceptable and accepted. This is what Chester Barnard meant when he said that leadership is the kind of behavior in an individual which inclines others to accept his guidance. Or, put in other words by Lyndall F. Urwick, "Leadership is the catalyst which transforms authority into power." *

Almost one thousand institutions grant degrees in business administration and management in our country today. This field of formal study is young indeed; it did not exist until the twentieth century. There is agreement that many matters pertaining to business and industry can be taught in the classroom, but whether or not a man can be taught in a classroom to be a supervisor or a manager is still strongly questioned. A man's potentialities for attaining a management position are

---

* Lyndall F. Urwick, "Management and Leadership," a speech delivered at Northwestern University (available in mimeo form from The Dartnell Corporation as "Talk of the Month," May, 1959).

based not as much on his technical competence or job know-how as on what kind of a person he is. Crawford H. Greenewalt, president of the Du Pont Company recently wrote: * "Contrary to accepted thought, the good manager manages quite as much with his heart as with his head; quite as much with instinct and intuition as with precise formulae."

On the supervisory obstacle course of "ability to execute," one of the biggest hurdles to get over is the attitude "If I want something done right, I have to do it myself." In this connection, Arthur C. Eckerman has proposed a new "law" which should eliminate this one outstanding hurdle and many of the lesser ones. His idea is based on the law of parsimony, sometimes confused with Lloyd Morgan's canon. The law of parsimony treats scientific data with the simplest available explanation of a function to be performed; Morgan's canon states that functions which can adequately be explained by concepts of a lower order should not be ascribed to a higher one. Although these doctrines apply principally to the biological sciences, Eckerman feels that they carry an idea which may prove helpful to leaders of men. In our own companies, he asks, how often do we see key men performing clerical work, keeping records, writing reports, checking up on minor activities, and making decisions for subordinates? What is it in human nature

* *The Uncommon Man*, McGraw-Hill Book Company, Inc., New York, 1959.

that makes us tend to escape into, or dwell on, the easier things, those things in which we feel confident and secure? Isn't it easy to show how the carrying on of work at a higher level which could be done at a lower level is expensive, inefficient, and disturbing to the morale of subordinates? If a supervisor cannot trust certain work to a subordinate which he feels he should not have to be doing, hasn't he a training job on his hands? If the company doctor tells him he's got to take it easier, shouldn't the supervisor do more supervising and less routine work? This is where Eckerman's new law of parsimony will help: "A supervisor should not perform a function which could be done by a member of his staff who is lower in the organization scale."

This may be painting with a broad brush, but let's see how we can fill in the details. Assuming that you are willing to accept (1) the definitions of *authority, power,* and *leadership,* (2) that the supervisory skills you need will not come to you through years in the classroom, and (3), last but not least, that you are willing to accept Eckerman's new law, what must you do to transform the supervisory authority vested in you into power?

1. You're not the swashbuckling, two-fisted character in *Annie Get Your Gun* who sang loudly, "I can do anything better than you." The chances are that you can, but you'll have to get used to the idea that someone else can do almost as good a job. Reconcile yourself to this fact! A task performed almost as well as you can

perform it is often adequate. The mere fact that someone else has done it will have saved you time for more
thinking, more planning, more delegating. This also
gives you more time to see that your subordinate is improving with each additional job he gets done. The day
will come when his completed job is as good as the one
you might have done.

2. See to it that your subordinates make their own
decisions. Let them skim their own judgments across the
pond and see where they hit. It's an easy thing for an employee to carry "half a decision" into the boss's office and
plant it there. If a weed should sprout, it's in the boss's
back yard. How comfortable and cozy for the employee.
This is habit-forming and dangerous. Why not have an
unwritten policy that no subordinate is to come to you
with a problem unless he presents a recommended
solution?

3. Augment your own confidence in your people;
don't diminish it. As your employees do more and more
jobs almost as well as you can, as they recommend solutions almost as good as your own, and as they learn to
get along more and more on their own, as you know you
can, reconcile yourself to the idea that you *can* have
confidence in them. How many times have you thought,
just before deciding "I can do it better than you," that
your subordinate was either too young or too old to
handle that job, too inexperienced or too old-fashioned,
too aggressive or lacking in follow-through, too intro-

verted or too extroverted, too darned undependable or too doggoned untrustworthy?

4. After you've gained the necessary amount of confidence in your employees, don't let them feel that if they don't know how to swim, you'll let them down. You can do this very easily by instilling fear and by excessive criticism. If they're too afraid and too severely criticized, they won't want to take any more responsibility. It's your job to be reasonable enough so that your subordinates will think and feel, "I'd do anything for that guy."

5. Don't fly without your altimeter. When a job has been assigned, set up control beams that light up your subordinate's path and serve as possible signals for you. Getting a job done can sometimes be as unpredictable as the weather. Of course, too many beams may prove that, again, you're doing the job yourself. This is the time for all good supervisors to change their tunes to "He can do something as well as I can."

6. Discover the individual differences among your men, but also recognize the needs all men share and learn how to satisfy them. A. H. Maslow of Brandeis University suggests that our basic human needs occur in an orderly, predictable progression. As soon as one need is satisfied, another takes its place. A man who hasn't eaten in three days is not likely to go out and buy a new suit, but when this man's hunger has been satisfied, he is apt to think of some clothes on his back.

Hundreds of surveys indicate that day-to-day, on-the-job needs will usually include the need for recognition, security, belonging, and interest in, and the feeling of, doing a worthwhile job. The supervisor who doesn't recognize these common-denominator needs will have a disgruntled, unsatisfied, griping group of workers. The supervisor who does satisfy these needs will find that his employees will then be ready to train and develop themselves without encouragement from the supervisor. These employees will crave more responsibility and will have the urge to identify personally and take pride in each piece of work they accomplish.

7. Create a positive personnel atmosphere, so your employees will feel properly induced to accept more delegated responsibility. "It doesn't make any difference whose job I do around here, I still get paid peanuts." "The boss tells me I'm his assistant, but he hasn't changed my job title in two years." "Why should I knock my brains out? Nobody around here gets promoted." Ever hear these familiar phrases? Tangible inducements such as pay increases are not always the answer. The important point here is that the guy who is carrying the load, the guy who has assumed the delegated responsibility in increasing doses ought to be provided with a positive personnel action, one that is important to him. Investments in these tangible and intangible recognitions will pay big dividends. The assistant supervisor who can attend a meeting in your place will feel

rewarded; the section head who can sign outgoing correspondence will feel recognized; the employee who is competent and dependable and was promoted will feel he is getting ahead. Remember, there are many inducements you can provide: a pay increase, a promotion, a better job title, better working conditions, and recognized status, occupationally and personally.

The art of delegation may be carried too far. Although one of the prime causes for supervisory failure is the lack of delegation, another cause for failure is delegating too much. What are the main supervisory jobs which should not be delegated?

1. One responsibility which should remain with the manager is the formation of general over-all policy established for his section, department, or division.

2. Another responsibility reserved for the manager is appraisal of his immediate subordinates. If the appraisal is not made by the employee's immediate superior, the effect of the appraisal is weakened and the chances for further employee development are diminished.

3. Disciplinary action to be taken with an immediate subordinate should also remain with the superior.

4. And obviously, one supervisory function which never is delegated is the promotion of an employee.

Why is delegation delicate? It is not easy to part with some of your authority and be left with full responsibility and total accountability for decisions made by others. Proper delegation requires keen insight, sound judgment, and sufficient skill on the part of the delegator. Too much or too little delegation must be placed on the scales and a balance between the two must be achieved in order to impart authority without losing control.

The manager who learns the art of delegation will benefit in many ways: He will be freed from the details of his work, he will find time to plan and control, he will enable his subordinates to learn how to make decisions, and he will have more time to receive his share of authority from *his* boss. This is a sure way to added vigor and progress for yourself, your employees, and your company.

# YOUR ORDERS

### beveled or sharp-edged?

### Giving orders

How do you give orders? This question developed as subject matter for discussion recently at a supervisors' meeting, and the results of the session were enlightening. If you're not able to fit yourself into one or more of the following descriptions, you'll find, perhaps, that many of them are descriptive of your boss.

1. *The satellite:* The supervisor, in orbit, who at light speed flies through the office or plant transmitting

short, quick quips about what needs to be done, not knowing if employee receivers are set on the right frequency.

2. *The pigeon feeder:* The supervisor who leaves a piece of work on your desk and expects you not only to eat it but to digest it while he's off feeding another pigeon.

3. *The gobbledygooker:* The supervisor who has taken many painful steps to explain in detail what needs to be done. He's the talking encyclopedia who at the end of a lengthy discussion brings forth from you, "Now I'm not quite sure I know what you mean."

4. *The warbler:* The supervisor who talks fast, eating his own words, and leaving you with the feeling that he has "marbles in his mouth."

5. *The ping-ponger:* The supervisor who moves from left to right, right to left, ordering, "Do this now. No, do this instead. Oh, do this now. No, do this instead." You're not sure which job will win out, but in the meantime your neck is sore.

6. *The big-time operator:* The supervisor often referred to as a B.T.O. He creates a steam bath of authority, and with back arched, chest forward, he keeps the boilers going. He's the boss who leans over your desk and remarks, "Of course, Jim, it's only a suggestion. Just let's not forget who's making it."

7. *The name dropper:* The supervisor who never gives an order of his own, as he is not part of the organ-

ization. All orders are commissioned in the name of the company president and on occasion for a member of the board.

8. *The do-it-yourselfer:* The supervisor who has four section heads but feels he must give orders directly to everyone in the department. This has the buzz-saw impact of conflicting orders, as the chances are that the supervisor doesn't know that one of his section heads requested something else only ten minutes ago.

9. *The egg collector:* The supervisor who puts all his eggs in one basket. He can rely only on Joe, and Joe therefore is the recipient of all jobs—big, small, tough, nasty, rough, heavy, light, and overtime.

Obviously, there is no ideal method of giving orders. The supervisor who acts as egg collector or warbler may still get his job done and therefore makes it difficult to generalize on this subject. Each supervisor usually develops his own method, and the proof of his ability to give orders can be seen and measured by the results he is able to obtain.

Giving orders depends on many variables, but especially on the personality of the man who is ordering and the personalities of those receiving the orders. The size of the crew, individual lengths of service, the pressures of the jobs, the number of males and females supervised, office or plant layout, and the time of day or week are some considerations which will determine how orders are given and accepted. But, in spite of these variables, there are techniques which can be utilized in order to improve your ability to give orders. These techniques, however, are almost totally dependent on your attitude to your people, your job, your company, and yourself. Without a healthy perspective, the quality and effectiveness of your order giving will suffer. Giving orders sets every job in motion. Kellogg writes that "The types of orders most supervisors are likely to give break down this way: the request, the suggestion, the command, the call for volunteers." *

Most of us are familiar with the request and will recognize it as the form most commonly used by supervisors: "Pete, when you have a minute. . . ." or "As soon as you've finished, will you. . . ." or "Pete, by the way, how's about. . . ." Most supervisors can accomplish what they set out to do by the use of the request. It's a pleasant, easy way of asking an employee to get a job done, especially with those employees who have been around for a long while and whose personalities are well in tune with that of the supervisor's. There are always employees who are excellent workers but who need to be treated with kid gloves. The request works well with them and doesn't rub their sensitivities the wrong way, as didactic demands from teachers or parents did years ago.

You may recognize the suggestion type of order as "Gee, Pete, we're supposed to get out ten units today

---

* Edward C. Kellogg, "Some Tips on Giving Orders," *Leadership on the Job,* AMA, 1957.

and we're behind a little. Do you think we can make up some time before quitting time?" Or "You know, the general manager may be around this afternoon. Do you think he'll say anything about the mess around here?" Or, "Do you think we're doing everything we can about keeping the records up to date?" This type of order, like the request, will accomplish a good deal for the supervisor, especially for his lead men and women. The suggestion will be immediately grasped by energetic, responsible, and ambitious employees; they like the feeling of having taken part in decision making. Their reaction will be one of "Yes, I think we'll be able to get all ten units out before closing time if we...." The suggestion type of order is probably least effective with your newer employees, and this is easy to understand. Your newer employees simply do not have the background of the department or may not yet have been adequately trained to be able to help come across with a sensible and practical co-solution. Nor will the power of suggestion make its mark on those employees who are undependable or incompetent; these employees just won't care and probably will come forth with such answers as "I dunno" or "Maybe" or "Don't ask me." The use of the suggestive order with your better people will have satisfying results, as ideas and countersuggestions will pop up that will have surprisingly high merit.

Sometimes the command type of order is the only way to get something done. This is surely the earliest form of order any of us will recognize. At home it was "Come here. Eat your spinach. Go to bed and stop biting your fingernails." At school it was "Sit up. Sit down. Go to the blackboard and stop talking in the rear." Commands from parents and schoolteachers were part of the process of growing up, and employees, now grown up, feel those days are gone forever. In fact, a command today is often met with bitter antagonism and defense mechanisms. Somehow or other, the command connotes a put-up-your-dukes attitude, and as your employee builds up resentment toward your command, he starts to boil at different degrees. This means he loses the meaning of your command and starts building up a sense of revenge. A simple rule to follow would be to avoid the command whenever possible, but remember to use it on those rare occasions when it is needed—for the mechanic who is off in the corner smoking a cigarette when he should be on the runway signaling the plane which has just come in for a landing.

In the Armed Forces, the tough sergeant has his own method of calling for volunteers: A smug look at his platoon accompanies a sour blast: "I want three volunteers, *you, you,* and *you.*" Needless to say, in this case, there is little choice. But asking for volunteer assistance in good supervisory form can serve as an exceptionally good type of order giving. This is handy in emergency situations, because most employees like the feeling of giving that something extra to the job; they want to help the other fellow. They find it easy to put themselves in the other fellow's shoes. This means that the supervisor must believe that people in general are interested not only in their own welfare but in what happens to other people; that they do care about the company and realize that what's good for the company is good for them too. There was a wise man who said, "Man does not live by bread alone, but by faith, by admiration, by sympathy."

### Better orders—bigger results

A specific way to improve an order is to be specific about the results you expect. When the size and speed of your orders are small and frequent and fall into a well-established pattern of expected results, it would be superfluous and tiresome to repeat the results you expect. As your orders become more important and are out of the normal routine of things, as a successful supervisor you will take time to review these distinct considerations:

1. What end result do you expect? Have you carefully considered it? Have you explained it specifically to your subordinate? In a brewing firm, Harry was told by his supervisor that maintenance costs were entirely too high and had to be cut. Several months passed by, and the maintenance costs were running about the same. The supervisor then told Harry that he wanted maintenance costs reduced by 10 per cent in sixty days. Two months later, Harry showed a 12 per cent reduction.

Why? The supervisor talked in terms of the specific rather than the general, in terms of results rather than activities.

2. Once you've analyzed the specific result you expect, think about the actions that can be taken by your subordinate—actions involving decisions without your constant approval. If Harry knows that you expect him to cut down 10 per cent on maintenance costs, how far will you go in allowing Harry to figure out how he's going to do it? When you know, let him know.

3. What are the chances of mistakes? How serious will they be? Many personnel and training specialists agree that for the up-and-coming employee, the correlation between his mistakes and growth is high. In other words, the employee learns through his errors and develops accordingly. The mistakes you predict or feel may feasibly occur should be discussed with your employee. Harry's supervisor did this before the sixty-day deadline became official.

### The proof is in the pudding

Mark Twain once said, "There ain't no way to find out why a snorer can't hear himself snore." There is a way to find out, however, whether or not your orders have been ordered. If the job is not getting done, you can be sure there's a fly in the soup and the chances are that it's in your soup bowl. Employees are not deaf and dumb. You may be at fault. How many orders did you give today? Are you satisfied with all the results? Can you think of one order you gave which netted poor results? When you gave that order, did you include these ingredients?

1. Speak clearly and at a reasonable pace
   *or did you "warble"?*
2. Assign a piece of work with a reasonable explanation of why, how, when, where, and what
   *or did you "pigeon-feed"?*
3. Be sure your employee understood what you told him
   *or were you "in orbit"?*
4. Be brief, direct, and to the point
   *or did you "gobbledygook"?*
5. Assign one job at a time whenever possible
   *or did you "ping-pong"?*
6. Forget your own importance as you would want your superior to forget his
   *or did you "big-time-operate"?*
7. Use your own legitimate and democratic authority
   *or did you "drop a name"?*
8. Work through your delegates instead of side-stepping them
   *or did you "do-it-yourself"?*
9. Be impartial and distribute orders fairly
   *or did you "egg-collect"?*

Did you give those orders unto others as you would like others to have given them unto you?

# 8

# YOUR REPRIMANDS

### *three-way vision*

Supervisors don't live on lonely desert islands, and supervisors are not hermits. Because we join hands with other employees in the business world and with friends and neighbors in a social world, we automatically surrender a part of our independence as we enter the area of harmonious human relationships. Here we see the signs "No smoking," "No cussing on the job," "Put trash here," and "No spitting on the floor." In every company there are basic rules that formulate disciplinary policy. You know them well, as they are fairly common; they deal with absenteeism, lateness, lunch periods, rest periods, and myriad rules and regulations most employees have come to know as *discipline,* a most unpopular word, since many of us think of it as the equivalent of punishment. Of several definitions in the dictionary, one reads, "Treatment that corrects or punishes"; another, however, reads, "Training that develops self-control, character, orderliness, and efficiency." The modern successful supervisor believes the latter definition. He knows that constructive and positive action rather than punishment will help him reach his objective of a self-disciplined team of employees.

As in every bushel, there's always the exception, and with this exception tough discipline may be the only answer. But, with good indoctrination, better training, and thoughtful supervision, the objective of self-discipline can be realized. The very word *discipline* comes from *disciple*—a follower. Your followers need a good leader, and as leader you have a direct bearing on the types of habits your employees form. Employees are not born with good or bad habits. They develop them at home, at school, and *on the job.* As a successful supervisor, you may be able to keep things calm and cool, but every once in a while one of your employees is going to disturb the atmosphere. Mistakes and errors can really cut into your productive output. Your nicely running schedule may go up in smoke because of repetitive and seemingly senseless errors. The best time to start correcting mistakes is the first day your employee reports for work. Then, keep it up as long as he is with you. When the same employee keeps making the same mistakes over and over again, it is an indication to you that additional training is needed. And investigate your working conditions, as they may be contributing to the number and frequency of errors.

Although W. E. Channing said that "Mistake, error, is the discipline through which we advance...", the successful supervisor must know when to take time and how to constructively help his employee learn as a result of that mistake. No one is ever free of making mistakes; no one will ever fully eliminate them. The reprimand can be a worthwhile tool for the supervisor if he knows how to use it. A day out of Charlie's life may sound familiar to you. Let's shadow him for a while.

Charlie left his apartment at 8:10 A.M. As he went past the front door, he overheard the super growl at the doorman, "George, if you're late one more time, I'll get that union to fire you!" Reprimand. At a luncheonette, while having a cup of coffee, Charlie listened as the store manager shouted to the waitress, "Dottie, once and for all, stop overloading that tray with dirty dishes. Ya want to break every dish again?" Reprimand. At an early morning meeting Charlie's vice president in charge of sales stuck his head in the conference room and barked, "Charlie, you may be sales supervisor, but I

wish to hell you'd tell me about these damn meetings.
You know the boss says there are just too many meetings
around this place." Reprimand.

Of course, Charlie's meeting was a dismal flop. He
simply couldn't keep his mind on what was going on.
Instead he took off in reverie and remembered that it
was only yesterday at a supervisor's meeting, in this
same room, that the subject of reprimanding was discussed. What was it that conference leader had said?
"Before you reprimand, be sure you get the facts." Yes,
that was it, and be sure you reprimand in private. And
avoid humiliating your employee. Charlie wondered
about the super: Did he really have the facts on George's
tardiness? And poor Dottie, the waitress: Did the store
manager have to blast her in public? And what about
me, thought Charlie, did JB have to humiliate me
that way?

### Getting the facts

When an employee breaks a rule or makes a mistake, put off your reprimand as long as you can and
use it as a last resort. It makes much more sense to look
high and low, far and wide, for the reasons why your
employee acts as he does. If you can remove the reason
without the reprimand, you'll make life easier for yourself and everyone else. Think of George and the super.
George's tardiness may have had nothing whatever to
do with his boss, the building in which he worked, or

his job. He may have had some problem at home. Perhaps his wife was ill that morning. Maybe she was pregnant. One of the kids may have broken a leg. True, all this may be of no concern to the super, but the super does want George to be on time. Did the super act as an understanding person? Does George feel he can't talk to the super? Was this the first, second, third time, or exactly what is George's lateness record? Did the super really know that George was late that morning?

Getting the facts in any disciplinary case is not as simple as it may sound. Here are some questions to keep in mind:

1. Were you actually present at the scene of the crime?
2. Did you accuse unfairly?
3. Have you talked to the employee to get *his* side of the story?
4. Have you checked the story from all angles?
5. Is your prejudice showing?
6. Was the mistake due to inexperience?
7. Had you given proper instructions?
8. Was the machine on the blink?
9. Should you check the employee's personnel record?
10. Should you reprimand?

Lester R. Bittel writes,*

As in most personnel problems, only a small percentage of workers cause disciplinary problems. People

* Lester R. Bittel, *What Every Supervisor Should Know*, McGraw-Hill Book Company, Inc., New York, 1959.

who break rules do so for a number of reasons—most of them because they are not well adjusted. One study of 4,174 discharge cases showed that 62.4 percent were for personal shortcomings of the employees themselves. Underlying personal characteristics that came up most were carelessness, non-cooperation, laziness, dishonesty, lack of initiative, lateness, lack of effort. The foreman's job as a result, is to help employees to be better adjusted. The record shows that people break rules less often in shops where the supervisor is a good leader, where he shows a sincere interest in his employees, where employees get more enjoyment from their work. After all, if an employee finds his work uninteresting and his boss unpleasant, is it surprising that the employee will find reasons for being late or for staying away from work altogether?

George could be one of these discharge cases. Wouldn't it have been better for the super, before his reprimand, to have gathered the facts?

### 'Tis better out of sight

A reprimand in public is like adding oil to the fire. The store manager, in Dottie's case, may not have known it, but he let the oil boil. He didn't remember, but that morning three new waitresses reported for work, and he really got off to a flying start as the curtain rose on Act One. He really made audience contact, and they reviewed and judged his performance. The consensus was that she was not guilty. Dottie achieved stardom in her role, and her attitude grew quite prima donna-ish. There

was a touch of the spitefulness in Dottie. The plot thick-
ened—the whole cafeteria staff lined up with Dottie.
All the other employees thought Dottie was right and
the store manager was wrong. As the curtain came down,
Dottie, the martyr, the star, was in the middle of the
stage bowing to an ovation.

How many stars have you created out of employees
whom you've reprimanded in public? One of the first
rules in handling reprimands is to handle them pri-
vately. Actually, it will bring about a greater effect of
discipline as far as the rest of the work force is concerned, since they will not know what has taken place
during the interview and may find it difficult to choose
up sides. Reprimanding on the spot will usually cause
you to lose control of your emotions, and in this case the
employee will gain the advantage. At times, a reprimand
on the spot will be necessary: If Dottie had slapped another waitress across the face and a referee had already
begun to call signals, action by the store manager would
have to be taken immediately. However, this was not the
case. Gather your facts and arrange for a reprimand in
private. This will be another step by which you will
get the most out of the reprimand, increase the over-all
effect of your disciplinary action, and take a long stride
in increasing the effectiveness of your supervision.

### Keep the employee's ego in mind

JB, in Charlie's case, had already committed two cardinal sins: One, he really didn't have the facts. Charlie

did try on several occasions to reach JB to tell him about the meeting, and he finally left a message with JB's secretary. Two, JB really cut loose in public and didn't know that, after he left the conference room, Charlie's friends, the other conferees, took pot shots at JB, none of which were very flattering. But what did all this do to Charlie? He was humiliated, and the boom had been lowered on his ego. If JB had thought things out, he may have decided that the reprimand was unnecessary. What a supervisor expects from his employees should be given careful consideration. This means considering the way the employee has acted in the past, how long he has been in the company, looking at the entire relationship between the company and the erring employee. Often, the sin committed is too small when compared to what is expected. Charlie couldn't help but feel humiliated by this contrast. And his ego just couldn't take it. It probably will take a while for him to forget "this little incident" and get back to an even-keel relationship with the boss.

It is a supervisor's prerogative to set up expected behavioral requirements from all his employees, but these should be delivered in simple, direct, straightforward terms. One area of faulty supervision is not letting the employee know what is expected of him. You, as supervisor, will be faced with letting employees know time and time again, and on occasion you will have to use the means of reprimand to gain this end. In order to accomplish this, you will have to keep the employee's ego intact. Your simple straightforward talk with him in private, pointing out what he did that was wrong in comparison with what was expected of him, will help redirect his efforts and make him understand why the reprimand was deserved. Smart-aleck criticism, one-sided off-the-cuff sarcasm, or a thrust at his ego will result in a tug of war, and can you say who will be the real winner?

### After the reprimand, what then?

The supervisor's role will almost always include follow-up action, and this is especially true after the reprimand has been made. If the employee handled his job incorrectly, you will want to arrange for additional training. You can do this yourself or delegate someone to do it for you. If the reprimand developed because of personal problems on the part of the employee, as an understanding supervisor you can arrange for some help, if not inside the company, then outside. The important thing here is for the employee to feel that positive action has been taken and that he as an individual has been considered. And this does not mean that you've reduced your reprimand to a tune on violin strings; it does mean you've been considerate, not condemning. Some companies require the supervisor to keep a record of all reprimands. These usually include noting what has taken place and when, the results of the discussion with the employee, and what steps will be taken to prevent similar occurrences in the future. Such records will also serve a purpose in the event additional disciplinary action is required.

### How are you on a reprimand?

Controlling an employee's performance is considerably more difficult than controlling the cost, quantity, or quality of your production. Broken machines can be repaired; a reduction in costs can be forced; a safety hazard can be removed; but how easy is it to correct an employee's bad habit? Discipline is at its best when it develops within the employee himself—when he voluntarily recognizes and practices rules, regulations, mature behavior, and above-average job performance. The intelligent manager does not confuse effective discipline with obedience through fear. Your ultimatums may work one, two, or three times. But the fear and force you create in this way will not bury employee unrest, dissatisfaction, and insecurity.

If you're a good supervisor, you're conscious of your employees. You know their idiosyncrasies, their ups and their downs, and you can probably foresee what trouble lies ahead and forestall it. If you're a weak supervisor, you're not as conscious of your employees as you should be, and your frequent reprimands are not helping you in your job. In either case:

Is your handling of the reprimand a constructive and positive action?

Does your employee know what he did wrong?

Does your employee understand the full implications of his error?

Does your employee know what can be done to avoid the same mistake again?

Does your employee feel that you've helped him?

If you can answer *yes* to all five questions, then you will probably agree with what Confucius had to say: "Wise man does not slip twice on same banana peel."

*9*

# PERFORMANCE APPRAISALS

## *a matter of coach, not couch*

In the nineteenth century Alexander Smith wrote: "The globe has been circumnavigated, but no man ever yet has; you may survey a kingdom and note the results in maps, but all the savants in the world could not produce a reliable map of the poorest human personality." Any careful observer must agree that, in any discussion of performance appraisal, these words have a special meaning in light of the serious resistance to conventional appraisal techniques by supervisors, managers, and other executives, in fact, by anyone who has to judge another human being. Some formal appraisal programs require the appraiser to delve into the component parts of one's personality. Even if it were possible to chart the contours of the poorest personality (or even the best), such a map comes dangerously close to a violation of the integrity of the human personality. Regardless of how much is known about personality, there is considerable evidence before us today that personality is not a thing to be torn apart and dealt with as a set of separable items but, rather, that it is a complicated net, elaborately woven with interacting and dynamic threads.

Among management men, there is considerable agreement that the godlike role of appraiser, rater, or evaluator is a difficult and distasteful one. All of us realize, of course, that management people must make judgments about their subordinates, for without such judgments there could be no logical and consistent salary administration, promotions, or transfers of personnel. However, the growing disagreement in administrative circles is not over whether the judgment is essential to sensible operation, but rather over the approach and underlying principles expected to be used and accepted by appraisers. Since some form of performance appraisal has become standard operating procedure in many firms (some companies fail miserably in this area one year and start all over again the next year), let's look briefly at the current picture.

## Why appraise?

Current performance-appraisal programs claim to be of benefit to *the company* in the following ways:

They aid management decisions in the matter of compensation including salary increases, bonus distribution, stock options, and promotional increases.

They assist management men in analyzing training and developmental needs, formal and informal, on the job and off the job.

They guide in the recruitment and selection of new employees.

They reveal for management certain organizational requirements such as the kinds and number of promotable and unpromotable men, the kinds and number of common and uncommon skills. In other words, they provide an inventory of human resources.

For the benefit of *the employee* (and this includes you), current appraisal programs claim to be of value because:

They tell him how he is doing on the job, where he stands, and what is expected of him in the future.

They give him a sense of being treated fairly when it comes to salary increases and other rewards and awards.

They help him know what he can do to climb to the highest rung of the ladder.

They give him an opportunity to complain, criticize, and gripe.

They give him an opportunity to express his personal goals, ambitions, and needs.

For you, *the boss,* current appraisal programs claim to help you in these ways:

They tell you whether or not your man is in the right job. If he's not, they can help you select his successor.

They help identify in your department the men who are the "go-aheads" and the "stand-stills," and also the "could-do-withouts."

They give you a fuller understanding of the jobs and goals of the department and a yardstick for measuring individual and group progress.

### How one company planned to use performance appraisals

The company decided it wanted a merit-rating plan. (Other companies may call it *performance review, progress report, developmental guide, appraisal report, evaluation review,* or *periodic review.*) Someone in the personnel department was given the assignment of working up the merit-rating plan suited to the company's needs and purposes. A plan was outlined and reviewed by some members of top management. A few changes were made. A meeting of supervisors was held to announce and "sell" the plan. Sample rating forms and a manual for merit rating were distributed. This plan, like water running down hill, was to start from the top down. The president was to rate those who reported to him. Each person he rated was to be called in for an interview, one at a time. The procedure called for ratings all the way down the line. The people rated by the president, in turn, were to rate those below them, and so on down to the messengers and the laborers. Each rating form was to be reviewed and countersigned by the superior's superior. Nonsupervisory personnel were to be rated semiannually, beginning at the individual's anniversary of his employment and every six months thereafter. Supervisory and executive personnel were to be rated annually also on individual anniversary dates. The results of the rating interview were to be summarized by the rater, and a copy of the completed rating form was to be sent to the personnel department for inclusion in the employee's personnel folder.

### Here's what happened

One month later: The president was to have rated two people that month as anniversary dates came due. One of the ratings was written; the interview took place. As the president had many things on his mind, he decided that the second rating and interview were not as urgent as some other pressing problems. Besides, he didn't like the results of the first interview. For a while there, things got rough, and he thought it best to go easy with his criticism of this particular vice president. At the conclusion of this first appraisal interview, he discovered something about himself—a normal dislike of criticizing a subordinate. He was gravely concerned about the "negative interview" and worried about his discomfort in telling one of his top administrators that he was only coasting along in the job. He also felt that this man was not any happier with the interview results than he was; he wasn't sure that this man *really* recognized or understood where he stood.

Two months later: At a staff meeting in the accounting department, the subject of merit ratings was brought up as follows:

DEPARTMENT HEAD: Jim, I'm sorry I haven't had a chance to talk to you about the rating, but according to procedure I'm to see Harry [the president] first. He's been busy but said he would get around to it as soon as he can.

CHIEF ACCOUNTANT: Well, Jerry, I went ahead and started on some of my people, and it just takes too much time. The paper work involved is tremendous. I really don't know what's to be gained by all this.

TAX ACCOUNTANT: I'm having a lot of trouble with the form itself, and I made a mess out of one of the interviews I had yesterday. It's a helluva job speaking out of both sides of my mouth. I told Chris he was doing a good job, but then I had to remind him that his reports were always late. When I told him to look into the Monday night course on "The Responsibilities of Supervision" at the University of Houston, you should have seen the look he gave me.

DEPARTMENT HEAD: Larry, you sent me the ten ratings on all your people, and they were just about the same for everyone. Who are you kidding? With all the trouble you've been having with Mike Mutecki, you left out some pretty basic points.

Six months later: The intuitive reactions to the merit-rating plan were gaining momentum and reaching serious proportions. Complaints were coming in from everywhere. Space prohibits a complete review of all the negative comments thrust upon the plan; in a paragraph, however, the antagonism might be summarized in this way:

The difficulty with the plan did not seem to be simply that raters were not flexible enough to meet a new procedure, or did not see a dire need for evaluating their people, or disliked a rating form as another piece of paper from personnel, or felt that the new plan lacked management support, or that they were dealing with abstractions, intangibles, and generalities. Their major concern was stepping into the judicial robe, that of judging the personal worth of a fellow man as if he were a physical object. They felt they were side-stepping the dignity of the human personality and ignoring the inherent worth of the individual. Under the principles of democratic leadership, was this newly devised rating plan honestly allowing the leader to *help* his followers?

Seven months later: The merit-rating plan was abandoned.

### Reflections

Have you been or are you in a situation similar to the one described above? You may wonder why this company's failure with a reasonably conventional appraisal program was discussed at such length. You, as a member of the management team, with the responsibility of directing organized human resources, must spend time making judgments about people and their jobs. This is so much a part of your responsibility that it may go on unrecognized from one day to another. You and other management members slowly or quickly, formally or informally, consciously or unconsciously come around to a feeling, and eventually a decision, that someone has "got it" and that someone else hasn't. The ability and capacity required in making judgments of people cannot be passed easily from one rater to another; it has a high correlation with one's ability to view the outside world clearly and objectively. It has to do with one's own self-confidence, level of intellect, and sense of security. No wonder it is one of the most important aspects and difficult tasks of your job. The next time you attempt to review the performance of one of your employees, check the validity of the following three statements:

1. The employee did what he could to summon the best evaluation he thought he could get.

2. He kept an ace or two up his sleeve and dealt the cards across the desk to his advantage (and why shouldn't he?).

3. At the conclusion of the evaluation process (and probably during it) the employee encountered a fork in the road, with one sign reading "Don't want to know about it" and the other "Please tell me all you can."

If you feel that the employee you appraised recently fits either or all three of these statements, you probably will begin to realize the "touchiness" of the appraisal situation. And, at times like this, you surely feel the pangs of the responsibility of your job. This chapter offers you no pat answers. There don't seem to be any. But the purpose of this chapter is not solely to examine an evaluation approach which usually fails but to provide you with an alternative suggestion which, with considerable practice, will enable you to overcome the pitfalls and distastefulness of the present appraisal method you may be using. In any case, it's worth serious consideration.

### Appraisals altered here

In 1954, Peter Drucker's book *The Practice of Management* took a deep dive into the philosophical depths of many management circles. One of Drucker's concepts made quite a splash; it is what he calls "management by objectives." Several companies, since the publication of this resourceful book, have cut through the waters and are finding a newer appraisal technique based on some fundamental social values. One of the goals in conventional performance appraisal methods is for the superior to effect some change in the subordinate's behavior. In this newer concept, a generalized principle would run like this: Allow the employee to examine his own reasons for wanting to effect a particular change. And let him examine his own motives. In this way, a change is more likely to be effected. Regardless of the power the superior may possess, it is still the subordinate who holds the reins of ultimate decision and action. After all, who actually decides for the mail boy whether or not he's to show up for work. No one but the private first class is responsible for being AWOL. It is the college junior who decides to cut the English literature class—no one decides for him. And it is the child who obeys or does not obey the parent.

Now let *us* take a deep dive into these partially explored waters, in order to take another and a newer look at employee appraisals so that we may understand certain fundamentals. There are five buoys, or principles, to guide us:

1. We should assume that the employee *knows more about himself* than the boss knows about him.

2. We should realize that what is *going to happen* is more important than what *has happened.*

3. We should understand that it is the *employee* who sets forth preplanned objectives *with the help of the boss,* and not vice versa.

4. We should try to put the accent on the employee's *strengths,* not his *weaknesses.*

5. We should accept the idea that the boss should be a *coach,* not a doctor with a *couch.*

When these five principles are applied, a new boss-employee relationship begins to develop. Appraisals then become the steppingstones to fuller employee development and increased boss satisfaction. And ultimately higher production levels will result for the company. It might be easier to analyze the five guiding principles by considering each from the employee's point of view and then from the boss's.

### Employee knowledge of self

*The employee:* It is assumed that the employee knows more about himself than any other person in the organization knows about him. He is capable of making his own judgments and evaluations in comparing his better qualities with his poorer ones. He understands more thoroughly the results of his upbringing and family background. He easily remembers his best subjects at school and those in which he failed. As he knew at the age of ten when to raise his hand to be excused, he now at age thirty-six knows approximately what it costs to support a wife, three children, a dog, and two canaries. He has the capacity to set his own goals and focus his sights on the road ahead. He knows how hard work will be rewarded by the company and of the satisfaction he will derive from it. He knows that the boss can help him succeed. If administered properly, he will welcome help from the boss.

*The boss:* It is assumed that the boss has a fairly good knowledge of what makes this employee tick. But, in spite of a voluminous employee personnel folder, various successes and failures on the job, the results of tests administered by an outside consultant or the company psychologist, ratings by other bosses, and outstandingly high production output, or a low sales record, the boss's knowledge of this employee is limited. Therefore, it limits the number and kinds of decisions he can make for this man. On the other hand, he can use what knowledge he has by helping the employee set realistic goals in view of the needs of the organization. He can set stakes along the way to test the soundness of such goals and the employee's plans for achieving them. His becomes a job of encouraging, listening, and developing rather than telling, criticizing, and deciding. And, most of all, he steps out of the judicial role. It's no longer a matter of appraising personal value, but one of providing for self-inspection on the part of the employee.

### The importance of tomorrow

*The employee:* It is assumed that the employee's awareness of what is going to happen, rather than what has happened, is of more value to the employee, the boss, and the organization. In preplanning objectives, it will make more sense for the employee to deal with how they may effectively be accomplished in the near future. With this look-ahead attitude, he can anticipate his trouble areas and perhaps overcome them before he reaches them. The employee learns by past experience, but knows also that it's a waste of time to cry over spilled milk.

*The boss:* It is assumed that the boss is also putting the accent on the future and that his evaluations are thus a means to a constructive end. The boss can use the employee's past mistakes in his teachings, but knows that yesterday's mistakes are *faits accomplis.* As the leader, he too should use his knowledge of previous mistakes in adjusting the stakes that outline a given course which the employee will take.

### Employee as preplanner

*The employee:* It is assumed that the employee, rather than the boss, will do all the basic thinking about his job and what steps he will take to get it done. A primary condition is that he have a job description available. (Many companies these days employ full-time job analysts for this purpose, but even a boss-written description will suffice.) The employee studies this, but makes it less formal by filling in more realistic details of the areas of his operation.

JOB TITLE: Builder representative, sales promotion.

JOB DUTIES: Promote the sale and use of bathroom equipment in new homes, housing developments, public buildings—search yellow pages for contractors, etc.; attend architects' meetings; study competitive merchandise this week; analyze last year's sales record in territory on Tuesday; etc.

With this living description, the employee can then make plans about the specific things he must do in the next three, six, or nine months. He may want to reorganize a series of reports, or he may want to take action to minimize sick-leave experience in the department. He may want to set up weekly staff meetings or prepare a series of fringe-benefit talks with his people. The important thought here is that definite statements are made about how and when these needs are to be satisfied. When the three, six, or nine months have gone by, the employee evaluates his accomplishments to date. The employee may realize that he has "lots more to offer" than he thought and in that case will probably tackle the next batch of goals with added zip and zest.

*The boss:* To set the record straight, one point in this new approach needs emphasis: Anyone who knows anything about managerial life should understand that the boss *is* boss. No organizational setup could exist without this phenomenon. In this discussion, it is mandatory to know that it is the boss's prerogative to turn thumbs down on any employee action; but if all goes well (and that is the objective of this approach), the boss will seldom exercize his thumb in this way. The boss will help the employee by reviewing the living description, the employee's self-evaluation, and the preplanned objectives, all in the light of organizational needs. The boss may modify or amplify the job description; he may add or subtract from its objectives. He will encourage the employee to go ahead when he knows that both he and the employee are satisfied with refinements that have been made. Three, six, or nine months later, he will take time to review actual accomplishments and perhaps again modify or amplify, add or subtract. The boss will feel that the employee really wants to please him and will go along with many of his suggestions. Like the employee, the boss too will feel he has "lots more to offer."

### "The good that men do. . . ."

*The employee:* It is assumed that the employee will enjoy this new role, because the emphasis is on the positive. He is not being judged about his weaknesses; no longer does he sit across that very long desk wishing he were off fishing with the boys or out looking for another job. No longer does he sit squarely on a checkerboard pattern, waiting to be moved left or right, skipped once or twice. He is the player himself, alive and active, figuring out his own moves (even with an occasional block), analyzing his own wrong plays, and trying to make up for them by wiser, more thoughtful actions.

*The boss:* The boss enjoys the positive approach also. No longer does he have to go through the grueling sessions of judging this man's personality, making negative suggestions, forcing decisions, and manipulating the employee's behavior to fit the company jigsaw puzzle. He feels satisfaction in taking the lead in helping this employee achieve not only his own ambitions but those of the company, as well. The boss begins to understand really what employee development can mean.

### Coach or couch

*The employee:* It is assumed that the employee "on the couch," during the conventional appraisal interview, is solving no problems, because he didn't ask to be there in the first place. The employee for years has believed that accepting and understanding a problem was half of solving it. While on the couch, he may be building more problem areas in antagonism of, disagreement with, and antipathy for the boss. Off the couch, the employee feels that no longer is the boss penetrating mystery motives, latent libido, or retarded relations. With the boss as coach, he knows that he is the star player on the field, carrying his own ball and aiming for a touchdown.

*The boss:* The boss steps away from the therapy table or couch and becomes the employee's coach. What psychological therapy does not require a tug of war over a personality issue? He knows that, as coach, he can make significant contributions to the player's skill and knowledge, to the success of the team as a whole.

### Some appraisal is better than none

A change from the conventional method of appraisal will surely take more time than overnight. Although the conventional method of appraisal is subject to criticism, it still can serve a useful purpose in furthering employee development. For a minute, let's return to our example, described earlier in this chapter, of the conventional company using a conventional appraisal technique. How might they have used this method to better advantage? The following points would have helped their management to increase their professional skills in appraising their subordinates:

### Provide time for weeding and cultivating

If the president of our anonymous company *can't find time* to appraise one of his executives, why should others find time? Talks with employees *do* take time, but think of the time such talks will save later on. If an employee is uncertain about something, such uncertainties must be weeded out or these uncertainties will grow into complex problems. Spending time on the development of employees will mean spending less time on day-to-day problems. This can only result in more time left for other work.

### Provide medicated treatment

Some appraisers in the company did have the time for appraisals, but they felt they didn't have to take the time because an employee who wasn't performing to full expectations would be soon, anyway. This is a matter of an unsolved problem solving itself, if not today, tomorrow. It's taking a look at a problem with eyes shut; or putting it in the closet, locking the door, and months later finding that it has disappeared. How can this be? Employee development must be looked at, studied, and stimulated. This is a job for one's superior. How can problems not get worse when they are kept under lock and key? An open wound or an internal tumor require medical treatment.

### Figure on facts

If you can find time and don't want sleeping dogs to lie, then be sure to figure on facts. This means preparing yourself in the following ways: reviewing your employee's job description and the performance targets that were set; determining how well the employee has met his performance goals; filling in the appraisal form in advance of the appraisal interview; documenting your memory and the form with details concerning the employee's experience, salary progress, work history; determining what you have done to guide the employee and what you have not done. Be sure the facts you have are objective; that opinions you have gathered from your own thoughts or others are not prejudicial.

### Set your goals

The tax accountant in our fictional company did not take time to set one or more goals in his appraisal interview with Chris. Shouldn't he have decided to (1) stimulate Chris to maximum effort, (2) let Chris know how effective he is in his job, and (3) help Chris work out specific steps for his improvement and development? Setting goals should include what is to be said to the employee. Although this is not always possible, the tax accountant could have outlined a course to be followed with Chris in exploring the areas of job effectiveness and job improvement. The tax accountant should have planned to avoid words like "errors," "mistakes," "lousy attitude," "stupid," and "weaknesses."

### Set your attitude on the right channel

A playback on the interview the chief accountant had with Jerry might have revealed that Jerry's attitude was pleasant but that the chief's was disgruntled. Remember, he kept complaining about all the paper work. Was the chief accountant really interested in Jerry? How friendly was he to him? Was he argumentative at any

time? Or did he just "run through the appraisal interview"? The chief's attitude was *not* helpful. This did
not help the success of the appraisal program, much less
Jerry's development.

### More reflections

Just as many seeds can join to make a full-bloomed
field of wheat, the multiplication of human accomplishments, no matter how small for any individual, will
create an organization—one that is strong in mind, fear-
less in spirit. The imposition of unnatural restraints, a
distrust in human dignity, a disregard for human
achievement—all surely lead to enslavement, a life mold
from which each of us was emancipated centuries ago.
Time and again, we have seen living proof that man,
given adequate encouragement, can find in himself un-
known avenues of performance. The most important
thing for you, in your job, is to bring into play the full
potential of all your employees, whatever may be their
station. Whether we speak of a department, a plant, a
local office, or a company, we know that actions hang on
conditions. Little in nature has the buoyancy of the human spirit; it is as sensitive to you and its environment
as the grains which crown the long, thin wheat stalk.
Your job and your challenge is to create an atmosphere
in which your employees, level of gifts notwithstanding,
gain positively through their association with you. Those
less gifted individuals will grow taller by the rule and

relationship with those more gifted. Inch by inch, they reach new heights of development, thus raising the over-all average of human achievement. The president of General Electric, Ralph J. Cordiner, once said, "Any sensitive observer must agree that the human potential in business has never been fully unleashed." * How true! How much of it is stored away in your environment? Now how about another go at an appraisal?

* Ralph J. Cordiner, *New Frontiers for Professional Managers,* New York, McGraw-Hill Book Company, Inc., 1956.

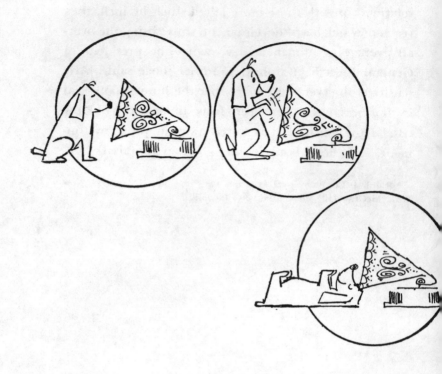

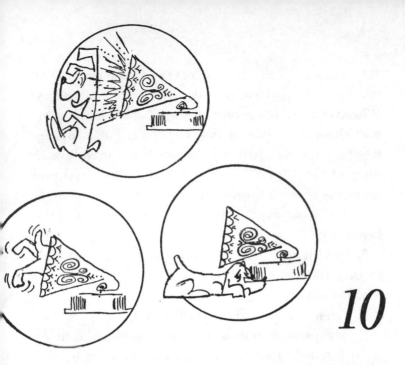

# YOUR LISTENING QUOTIENT

### in one ear and out the other

Can you recall the aural round-robin game played by school-age youngsters who sat in a circle? An appointed leader would start the round by whispering a sentence to a friend on his right, and this friend would whisper the sentence to someone at his right, and so on. The last one in the circle would repeat the sentence out loud. The leader would then repeat the original sentence, and everyone would laugh, because it was so different from what the first person had said. Does this child's game remind you of experiences in the plant, office, or factory? Wherever there is a group of people, there is also a human chain of people talking to people, but a message flowing along this chain may be grossly distorted because many of the "links" are poor listeners. Have you ever heard any of the following expressions?

1. You look upset! You don't hear a word I'm saying.

2. I've listened to every word you've said, and I absolutely agree with you.

3. Do you get the gist of it?

4. You haven't heard a word I've said.

Each expression tells a story of a person who hasn't really listened. This person may at some time be you. Supervisors today are beginning to find that communication with their employees, superiors, and peers depends more and more on the spoken word than it does on the written word. They are also discovering that the power of the spoken word depends not on how people *talk* but on how they *listen*.

Let's listen in on Willie (sectionhead, shipping) and Jim, (supervisor—mail, shipping, and receiving). The words in italics are Jim's thoughts.

### *"You look upset. You don't hear a word I'm saying."*

WILLIE: I'm sorry to bother you, Jim, but the wrong order was sent out to Blake's on Friday.

JIM: *Wrong order! Not another one. I just can't take it any more.*

WILLIE: Friday was a real busy day and five cartons were sent, but they were the wrong materials.

JIM: *I was scared stiff last month. I'm sure to get the ax on this one.*

WILLIE: I found out about it early Sunday morning, and naturally I later sent out the right stuff.

JIM: *What will they do to me? And two weeks before Christmas. This just can't happen to me.*

WILLIE: It took me all Sunday afternoon. No kidding, Jim, I looked through four or five hundred cartons before I could find the Blake order.

JIM: *Why does this always happen to me? How will I explain it?*

WILLIE: I told the guys in the Shipping Room that I'm not paid to play detective.

JIM: *The car isn't paid for.*

WILLIE: I'm getting sick and tired of this. I questioned each guy. I had to find out who made the mistake. I spent over an hour with them this morning and I really gave them the business.

JIM: *I'm so mad I can't see straight.*

WILLIE: I'm pretty sure it was Robinson who flubbed, and this is not the first time.

JIM: *Mistakes! Mistakes!*

WILLIE: What are we going to do with him, Jim? Blake's our biggest customer, and this can't happen again.

JIM: *Why didn't you do something about it, Willie?*

WILLIE: Now I've talked to Robinson at least three times about this, and it just goes in one ear and right out the other.

JIM: *What shall I do? I'd better call Blake's right away.*

WILLIE: It was only last month that the same thing happened and—What's the matter, Jim? What's wrong? You really look upset. You don't hear a word I'm saying.

Poor Jim. He was upset. He hadn't heard a word Willie said. As soon as he heard the words "wrong order was sent," he closed his ears. He didn't want to hear any more. Jim's listening ability was reduced to almost zero because he was emotionally upset. Wendell Johnson, in his article "The Fateful Process of Mr. A. Talking to Mr. B.," * wrote that, in different degrees and in many different ways, listening ability is affected by our emotions, that we mentally turn off what we do not want to hear. At times, our emotions in effect cause deafness. Nichols and Stevens wrote † that

> If we hear something that opposes our most deeply rooted prejudices, notions, convictions, mores, or complexes, our brains may become overstimulated, and not in a direction that leads to good listening. We mentally plan a rebuttal to what we hear, formulate a question designed to embarrass the talker, or perhaps simply turn to thoughts that support our own feelings on the subject at hand.

Each day in our jobs we may be greeted with news for which we are emotionally tuned in some way. How well

* *Harvard Business Review,* January-February, 1953, p. 49.
† Ralph J. Nicols and Leonard Stevens, *Are You Listening?* New York, McGraw-Hill Book Company, Inc., 1957

we can monitor the emotional wavelengths of such news will in large part determine how well we listen.

### "I've listened to every word you said, and I absolutely agree with you."

Late Saturday evening, the chief maintenance man informed one of the electricians in his department that he would have to report for work on Sunday. The electrician angrily said that he had his "bellyfull of Sunday work" and would not work on Sunday any longer. The chief maintenance man gave him an argument and told him he'd better be in the plant at 7:00 A.M. sharp on Sunday morning. The electrician glared at him, told him that he'd have a "long wait coming," and walked away. The chief maintenance man (the talker in this dialog) walked directly into the supervisor's office, told him the story (the supervisor is the listener here) and added:

CHIEF: I suppose I should have waited until he calmed down, but he ought to know that we need him.

SUPERVISOR: *I'll be in tomorrow myself.*

CHIEF: I finally had to warn him that he'd be suspended for one week without pay if he didn't show up. After all, he doesn't have the right to decide whether or not he's to work overtime.

SUPERVISOR: *You're right, that's your decision.*

CHIEF: It's true, though, he has worked often on Sundays and really hasn't given me too bad a time. But he knows that a lot of maintenance work must be done when the rest of the plant is not working.

SUPERVISOR: *We can get a lot of things done on Sundays.*

CHIEF: That's the nature of his job. And the work this Sunday is important, even if we do it only once a year.

SUPERVISOR: *I like this boy. He's got good ideas. I put him in this job—that was a pretty good choice I made. No question about that.*

CHIEF: I'm going to change the oil in the mill line breakers —and tomorrow is the best time to do it. I can't do it by myself. I need at least two to help me out. I asked three other guys to help out, and they all had excuses.

SUPERVISOR: *Some people always have excuses. People today are funny. It's not like the good old days. We thought fifty-six hours a week was nothing.*

CHIEF: I can't see why he had to make a fuss. He didn't even give me a chance to explain why I needed him. Sure, I could have told him earlier in the week, but I was pretty busy and just didn't get around to it. Whaddya say? Are you going to go along on the week's suspension without pay if he doesn't show up?

SUPERVISOR: I've listened to every word you said, and I absolutely agree with you.

This supervisor not only opened up his ears, but he accepted every word from the chief maintenance man, regardless of what was really behind the incident. Was he anywhere sure of what the chief was telling him? Probably not, because he was hearing exactly what he wanted and liked to hear. He opened his listening gates wide and let the whole flood of events, some true, some questionable, come through. Did the supervisor ask any intelligent questions? No. He firmly believed in over-

time, especially on Sundays. This was his code. He remembered the good old days. He might have asked why
the chief didn't plan Sunday work earlier than late Saturday evening, especially if the job to be done is done
only once a year. The supervisor might have questioned
why some men got away with excuses and others didn't.
But this supervisor felt comfortable during this conversation, and any critical powers he possessed were immediately put aside, because the emotional springs
touched off by what he heard sent him flying high in the
sky.

### "Do you get the gist of it?"

When Dominick, a new supervisor of the finishing
department (the listener) in a clothing plant, was transferred to a department that had long been a sore spot,
Harry, the outgoing supervisor (the talker), told him
about one particular worker. The man in question was
Salvatore, who seemed to have a lot of influence over
the other workers and probably was partly responsible
for the low output in the department.

HARRY: Yep, I guess Salvatore is a problem in some respects,
but I think you'll be able to do something with him.
The other day, one of the other pressers gave me a blow-
by-blow description of what Sal was up to last week.
DOMINICK: *Salvatore is a problem.*
HARRY: On Monday, Sal refused to underpress trousers.
DOMINICK: *On Monday, he refused to underpress trousers.*

HARRY: That afternoon he left the floor and went downstairs for coffee, or maybe a beer. But he did ask my permission.

DOMINICK: *Salvatore went off for coffee or beer.*

HARRY: On Tuesday he made four or five personal phone calls. They say she's quite a doll.

DOMINICK: *Salvatore makes personal phone calls. How many did he say? Salvatore was ten minutes late. Was that on Tuesday or Wednesday?*

HARRY: Oh yes, that day he was ten minutes late from lunch, but he had to go downtown to get his chest X-rayed. The next day, Wednesday, he was ten minutes late, but he hasn't been late in quite a while. You should get along with him okay. I hear you're pretty good at making friends. But on Thursday, someone said he talked too much, and Sal said as long as he was getting out the work, what was the difference.

DOMINICK: *Salvatore is a talker.*

HARRY: After all, this isn't a prison.

DOMINICK: *Was he or was he not getting out the work?*

HARRY: Sal's not a bad egg. I think he needs a pal. Keep an eye on him and see what you can do with him. Do you get the gist of it?

DOMINICK: Sounds like a real problem case to me. Would you have fired him?

Giving and receiving facts in oral communication is an everyday occurrence on the job. We couldn't get along without them. But the new supervisor listened only to facts and did not get the gist of this conversation. Perhaps his newness to the job caused a certain amount

of undue anxiety in talking things over with the outgoing supervisor, but at any rate he missed the main
issue about Salvatore. In trying to remember the details
about Salvatore's behavior, the new supervisor neglected
to catch the full impact of what was being said. In this
case, the facts came at him so rapidly that, at the end of
the conversation, he wasn't sure he had caught them.
Was Sal ten minutes late on Tuesday, or was he ten minutes late on Wednesday? The new supervisor was concerned with pieces of the pie, when he should have been
listening to the whole. This factual gathering resulted
in a loss of the *idea* that Salvatore could be handled by
the right person and that the right person could well be
the new supervisor.

### *"You haven't heard a word I've said!"*

All of us know how easy it is to talk. All of us, by talking, at one time or another, have put the world in shape
at a cocktail party, at yesterday's conference, at a nearby
luncheonette counter, in the rest rooms, or at a twenty-
five-year-association meeting. But most of us will agree
that listening is much more difficult; it really takes a lot
more concentration. It's more difficult than a telephone
conversation, a gab session, a memo to the boss, a letter
to a friend, telling off an employee, asking for a favor—
more difficult than almost any other form of personal
communication. Let's listen with the fellow who has hit

the ball way out in right field, run all the bases, and
scored a home run while the right fielder has not yet
caught the ball.

BOSS: (speaking very slowly) Management has finally approved plans for a company-wide orientation program
for all regular and temporary employees. They really
spent quite a bit of time talking about it.

ASSISTANT: (listening intently, but getting impatient with
the slow rate of speech; thinking very quickly) *Oh, I
must remember to tell him about Morrison's call. He'll
surely want to know about it.*

BOSS: And I might add that they have very specific ideas as
to what they'd like to see done. For example, they want
the company colors to be used in any print job, and
they want the print shop to do it in the Atlanta plant.

ASSISTANT: *The estimate on redoing the basement was just
too high. Mary thinks it's a fair price, but I'd better get
another bid. I could get him to quote less, but I don't
want that bar to be any narrower than 22 inches. That
vinyl floor is darned expensive. I probably could do
it myself, but you know Mary—*

BOSS: They want some copy and art work to be ready by the
first of the month. That's a little more than three weeks
from now.

ASSISTANT: *—She wants the experts only. Well, maybe she's
got a point. The floor in the upstairs closet doesn't look
too hot, but after all, it was my first try.*

BOSS: They even go so far as to talk about regional managers'
and supervisors' meetings in order to get the program
across.

ASSISTANT: Uh-huh.

BOSS: What did you say?

ASSISTANT: Unh-unh.

BOSS: Oh, I thought I heard you mumble something. Find the copy we had prepared three months ago for the quarterly personnel meeting, and we'll take a look at it again the first thing in the morning.

ASSISTANT: *I'm not sure I like the black bar top. That guy really didn't explain the difference between Formica and Micarta. The kids like it, though. The lights flush with the ceiling are really gonna be something.*

BOSS: And will you call Val Senti and ask him to come in. He'll have to give us a dummy layout in a hurry.

ASSISTANT: *But what about light over the bookcases. They go clear up to the ceiling. A lamp won't do, but we could throw a small spot on the bookcases and the fish tank. Let's see now, in about three months it will all be....*

BOSS: Bill, I swear! You haven't heard a word I've said!

One reason why listening is so difficult is that people think faster than they talk. A secretary who can take dictation at 125 words a minute is considered to be an excellent stenographer. Not many people talk at a greater speed. Although the human brain, in many instances, is still a great mystery, we do know that catching 125 words a minute while listening is a snap job. The brain catches the spoken word so quickly that it actually has hundreds of "recess periods" in between spoken words. How well the listener can concentrate on the spoken word will determine how good is his listening ability. Most minds, after catching the spoken word, will wander from it but quickly come back again to pick up and hang on to the next few words. If this is accomplished, the understanding of what has been said will be high. The poor listener will usually wander off far afield and forget to come back in time. One might say that he gets carried away with his own thoughts. The assistant above only half listened. He wandered frequently and was away too long. The chances are that he heard less than half of what was said.

As a supervisor, listening well may spell success or failure in your job. Mistakes because of faulty listening compound themselves as easily as other errors. As a co-operative and well-liked supervisor of people, it's easy for you to say off the cuff, "C'mon in, Joe. Let's talk about it," but *once Joe is in,* are you listening to him? Once an employee knows that you're "the kind of guy who doesn't listen," he'll fail to come to you with things, important things, that you should know about. If you don't listen to what's said up the line, you won't get the gist of it, either. A problem that you don't know how to listen to can grow more troublesome each day and may ultimately cause your otherwise unnecessary downfall.

There are a few simple things to concentrate on in order to improve your listening ability:

1. Try to understand the major points being made by the talker. Fight off immediate conclusions that you may come to, until the talking is over. Then review the gist of what has been said.

2. As we listen, we have preconceived ideas about what is being said. Naturally, we think we're right in everything we think and feel. Some say this is human nature. But if you hear something that challenges your belief, hang on to it too, for there may be some truth to it, and this will lead to a fuller and better understanding of what has been said.

3. Since you will think faster than words are delivered to you by the speaker, make full use of the recess periods that seem to be inevitable. You can do this in a number of ways. Some suggestions are: Try to figure out what the talker will say next; weigh carefully any facts that are presented, but don't try to memorize isolated facts; look directly at the talker, as his face will give additional signs of what he's trying to get across; listen attentively to his inflections of speech, the melody of his voice—when does he bellow and on what words, and when and what does he whisper?

Listening well is only one part of the successful supervisor's job. Your ability to listen attentively, whether it be at home or on the job, may not solve your major problems, but it can lead the way to minimizing the human frictions that you encounter each day.

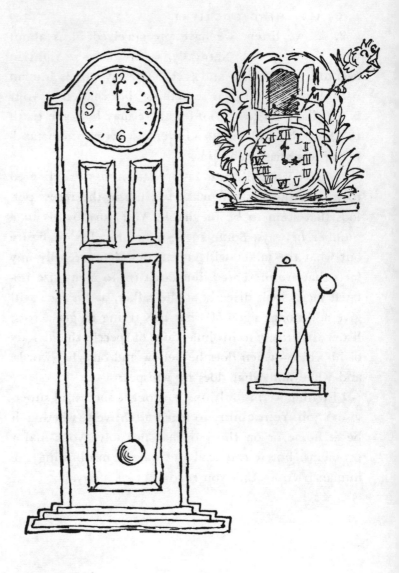

# 11

# YOUR TIME

### *how's your hourglass?*

Webster defines an hour as "The twenty-fourth part of a day; sixty minutes." Your boss defines it as "One-seventh or one-eighth of your workday, which costs your company three, four, five, or more dollars for services which may or may not have been rendered." Regardless of the frame of reference, of one thing we can be sure: time consciousness is here to stay! Everywhere are time clocks, stop watches, wrist watches, church bells, and noon whistles. Today's living is paced with an invisible metronome, a tick-tocker of costly time passing by. Let's face it—you are judged not only by quality but by quantity, not only by productivity but by its speed. Turn back the hands of your clock, and you'll easily recall that one of the first things you learned was to tell time. Once you could tell time, your metronome was set in motion. At school, at a dance, on the ball park, in the Air Corps, your actions were marked in seconds, minutes, hours, days, weeks.

Today, at 11:45 A.M., you'll say, "My gosh, it's already lunch time," and at 5:30 P.M. you'll say, "Darn, where did this day go?" Finding the time to get everything done is a problem facing most supervisors. You can solve it by organizing the hours you have available on the job. Seven hours, not eleven. Eight, not twelve. All right, make it eight and a half. Let's look at this organization of time by three simple actions: (1) planning your work; (2) delegating definite responsibilities and authorities; and (3) finding and using short cuts. Then ask yourself whether or not you *are* getting the most out of every hour.

### Planning

There must be madness in the methods used by everyone you work with, for your job is certainly not made up of an orderly inflow of assignments. Sometimes the work sky is a clear Caribbean blue, no clouds, no wind. Sometimes when it rains, it pours, all lightning, more thunder. But it's up to you to take these work assignments off the belt line and process them. Put first things first. With some analysis, the hurdles in accomplishing assignments become transparent.

*Solo planning session: late Friday afternoon.* After you beat your fist on your desk top wondering where the week went, close your office door and simmer down. If you don't have a calendar which shows a week at a glance, get one, for you'll want to plan the coming week. You can plan this in fifteen or twenty minutes. Think ahead. But don't plan every minute, as you'll need some time for the emergencies. List what you want to accomplish the following week, and it's not a bad idea to be a little specific and say that this will be done by Monday afternoon and that will be done by Tuesday morning. List the important things first, and then fill in with the secondary chores. When Monday morning rolls around, it won't be as blue as you thought, as you know what's got to be done. Knowing what needs to be done will save hours, and you'll want to follow through by working your plan after you have planned your work.

*Inner-sanctum progress report: end of the month.* One monthly check-out session after four Friday afternoons is in order. A monthly progress report, twelve times a year, can be a real timesaver. You can devise one to suit your own needs. Don't forget to keep score. Don't worry if only 50 per cent of your objectives were met the first week. As the weeks go by, your batting average will improve. Why? Because you're organizing your thoughts and thinking through your assignments.

A monthly progress report also can be very helpful in

guiding your subordinates and keeping your boss informed:

"Look, Joe, you did a good job last month. Ninety-five per cent of the drawings for the Stamford job were sent out on schedule. Thanks for your help."

or

"You see, sir, although we added three new replacements last month, we still were able to improve on the number of drawings we sent out on the Stamford job. We're up to 95 per cent."

*Midstreaming or streamlining?* The old adage about changing horses in midstream, the loud shouts of "Hold that line," and the quality of stick-to-itiveness all have found places in the realm of common sense. You've seen the fur fly, the ruffled feathers, and the Calamity Jane who just can't stick to one job until it is reasonably completed. How many times have you task-hopped to the point that at the end of the day nothing has been accomplished, nothing neared completion? Think of the times you have sat in someone else's office, time set aside to solve one simple problem, but that someone behind that desk jumped from numerous telephone calls to various bits of instructions to his secretary or assistant and even to a brief visit to the men's room. You left that office with no answer, no solution, no plan. If you're midstreaming, then it's time to save time by streamlining. Tackle one job at a time, and stick to it. Insist in your own mind that you get it done, and get it done before moving on to the next job. Sure, there'll be interruptions which can't be helped, but if you tackle hard enough, you'll be able to lay many completed jobs aside, saving many minutes and hours and leaving a fulfilled day behind you.

*Or are you Jack-be-quick?* Imagine the task confronting Darwin as he formulated his *Origin of Species.* The slow, almost unending task of collecting bits of information and classifying it. You may not be devising a new origin of species, but each day in your job you are collecting various pieces of work which have originated from various species. The wise supervisor will not only collect his tasks but will sort and grade them. Doesn't it make sense and save time to handle most of your dictation at one time? Doesn't it save the stenographer's or secretary's time also? Isn't it wiser to put aside ten or fifteen minutes in the morning and in the afternoon to make all phone calls? How about signing all outgoing mail toward the end of the workday? How about set hours for talks, chats, and interviews with your employees or other company and outside people? "Salesmen interviewed 10:00 A.M.–12:00 in the purchasing department," "Applications accepted in the personnel department 10:30 A.M.–1:00 P.M.," "Window closed," and "Coffee served 9:30–10:00 A.M. in the cafeteria" are signs you see each day. These people in these areas have certain jobs organized. Time has been set aside to get something specific accomplished. How many signs are written in your mind?

*Tackle and tickle.* We all accept the fact that no human being can remember everything, any time, anywhere? May we accept, too, the fact that most supervisors have a hundred and one items to pay attention to? Then the question is how time can be saved in remembering to pick up things where they had to be left off. "Tackle, then tickle" is one answer. If you've done everything you can on a given task and it has to be put aside for future action, devise a method for reminding yourself that this needs to be done. Filing it under *F* won't help. One method can be as good as another, if it works. Attractive folders are sold in most stationery stores for follow-up, or tickler, purposes. A simple folder having jackets for each day of the month can easily be used for placing material which will have to come up on the fifteenth or twenty-first of the month. Files in a double drawer in your desk, each having a set reason for being there, such as "To be dictated," "For monthly sales meeting," "Ideas I would have liked to have dreamed up," "Supervisor's manual on company policies," and "For supervisors' meeting" are some good examples. A workable filing system is a necessity. Have a place for everything, and keep everything in its place. Whether you use a loose-leaf binder or a six-drawer legal file cabinet, you must be able to find it when you want it.

### Delegating

In a sprinkler system, the work load is distributed. The golfer has his caddy, the waiter has his bus boy, the bowler has his pin boy, and the supervisor has his staff. Employing the art of delegation will in itself save you valuable hours. And, remember, the art of delegation includes passing along some of the authority. At the end of this day, ask yourself how well you delegated. Did you assign specific responsibilities to others? "Joe, you do all the checking out, and, Alice, you process all retail orders." Did you, yourself, take care of the most important jobs? "I hired a new foreman today, merit ratings were completed, and the cost figures for job T22 went out on time." Are the routine tasks easily and quickly handled by members of your team? "Bill, you handle the weekly absentee reports, and, Pete, each morning you pick up the order sheets from production." And most of all, ask yourself: "Do I still think that the only way anything can get done is to do it myself?"

### Short-cutting

Most of us know that the shortest distance between two points is a straight line. How often this theorem is applied in your day-to-day activity will be measured by the amount of time you save. Have you ever left your office to go to the engineering department or any other department for an immediate answer you needed and found that you forgot what you wanted when you finally got there? Of course, in the meantime, you checked in on the weather with Charlie in purchasing, described last night's miracle of driving home on that icy road to Marty in operations, and planned Sunday's golf game with Sam in the meter department. Actually, you could have saved that hour and used just the time required to follow the straight line by making a simple telephone call. Person-to-person contacts often are a necessity, but usually a quick phone call makes it easier for both people concerned. After all, someone else's metronome is ticking away faster and faster all the time, too.

Talk may be cheap, but it is a time consumer. Everybody likes to talk, and the time-conscious supervisor should get in the habit of writing short memos instead of talking so much. You can put down briefly in writing what is needed and when, what has been done and why. If a memo isn't required, you can always call on the phone.

Someone once said that there are two great stigmas on the twentieth century: one—traffic, two—paper work. I'd like to add a third—meetings. It seems as if any time you ask someone where he or she is going these days, on or off the job, the answer is "to a meeting." No one can question the necessity of meetings in which information is obtained or given or where a problem is solved: such meetings have proved their worth as excellent methods of communications. But what about those meetings which leave their participants feeling "what a waste of time!"? If meetings you attend (either as leader or conferee) eat up your time, you should appraise your meeting behavior. Did you prepare yourself *before* the meeting? Did you meet the subject head-on or did you go off into outer space? How much did you gobbledygook? Did you listen attentively? Did you give a little, take a lot? How high was your quibble quotient? Did you solve your problem or merely schedule another meeting?

If you know someone who has the reputation of being a good supervisor and one who gets things done, the chances are that he has found the many short cuts in his daily routines which have helped build this reputation.

Benjamin Franklin did not have you as a supervisor in mind, but his words apply: "Dost thou love life? If so, don't squander time for that's the stuff life's made of."

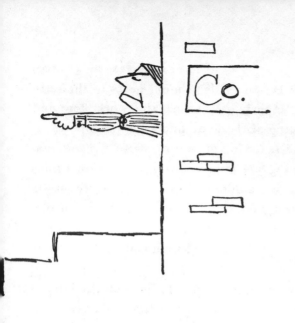

# *12*

# PROBLEM EMPLOYEES

## *a problem with problems*

"It seems that everybody is queer except thee and me," the elderly Quaker spake to his spouse, "and sometimes I think thee is a bit queer." In many chapters thus far, we have discussed human behavior on the job and have tried to understand it. But what about employee behavior which we feel we must change, control, and direct in order to meet specific needs in our work situations? Is all employee behavior in a given department "normal," or do some employees act in odd and different ways? Do all of them mesh gears to the satisfaction of the supervisor? Or are the work flow and general well-being of the department ever hampered or blocked by the behavior of one or more difficult employees? The range of descriptions of the "normal individual" is vast, and seldom will two people agree on the same definition. Often, the "average" employee for one supervisor is the "offbeat" for another. What are some typical employee problems, and what can be done about them?

Many surveys have shown that failures on the job are more often attributable to personality maladjustment than to any other single cause. Of the significant areas in which most people meet life's daily problems and learn to relate to other people at home, in school, in church, in social circles, and on the job, life on the job has probably received the least attention from sociologists, psychologists, psychiatrists, personnel men, and management people. Yet, it has been said that one universal characteristic of the supervisor's job will be his problem with his problem employees. Normal or offbeat, some of your employees require special consideration. We cannot identify all of them in one chapter, nor can we set forth all the techniques you can use to change, control, and direct employee behavior. But let us try to make a start.

Bill Wood, nephew of William C. Wood, president of Wood and Company, Inc., a medium-sized but well-known textile firm, sat under a big oak and watched more than eight hundred employees cavort and carry on in the Wood spirit on their annual picnic. The picnic grounds smelled of spring, hot dogs, and beer. Bill Wood, only thirty-three years old, was heir apparent, sure to be president of Wood and Company, Inc., in two years. Bill was no newcomer to the business. His uncle had seen to it that he joined the Wood organization immediately after college. Bill knew most of the Wood employees, many by their first names.

There was Pat, today's baseball star. He had just hit a home run. On the job, he put in a lot of overtime, but he was late almost every other day. People liked Pat. Pat had almost ten years of service. Pat is a pretty good egg, thought Bill, but why was he such a *latecomer?*

Doris was having a third doughnut with a third cup of coffee. Everyone had abandoned the lunch tables an hour ago, but Doris sat there, by herself, forgetting the many pounds she should leave behind her. The company's sick-leave policy was liberal and appreciated by a majority of employees. Doris appreciated the policy, too, in a special way. She took every day she thought "she had coming to her," whether she was feeling well or unwell. Bill Wood remembered that two months ago her supervisor brought her absenteeism record to his attention. For each year since her employment, Doris had taken the full amount of sick leave in either one-, two-, or three-day absences. At this stage of her eligibility for sick leave this meant the equivalent of nine weeks off at full pay. When on the job, Doris was a good worker, but why was she such a *sick-leaver?*

Bill Wood looked past Doris and the lunch tables, and his eyes rested on Ted. Among a clique of employees, he could see half a dozen white paper cups, each receiving double shots of Four Roses from the hand of Ted, a self-appointed bartender. Ted was in the shade, as on all picnic days, yet his face had that certain red glow not usually associated with an overdose of sunshine. Ted Thompson, or Mr. Moonshine, as most other employees called him when he was not in hearing range of their words, could drink anyone under the table at any time. He was proving his point at this moment. He proved it yesterday and last week. He has been proving it for years. Often a good salesman, thought Bill Wood, but what a problem. Why was he such a *heavy drinker?*

Agnes, or Aggie, as everyone called her, was holding her own next to Ted's. Aggie drank only on picnic days; the rest of the year she was on the wagon. On the job, she walked and talked. If you couldn't find Aggie at her machine, you might try shipping, receiving, accounts receivable, or ac-

counts payable. When you found her, you would
hear her recital of yesterday's lovely wedding cere-
mony, today's coffee prices, or tomorrow's sale at
the Salvation Army. When at her machine, Aggie
was considered a good worker, but why, too much of
the time, was she a *walkie-talkie?*

Tony was the afternoon's catcher. Behind his
catcher's mask was a strong, dark face with tragic
lines. Hired late in life, Tony had a considerable
number of gripes. He voiced his negative opinions
about the company's vacation policy and his fellow
employees, and claimed there weren't enough pic-
nics. If his team lost the day's game, he would be
the biggest and best griper. Tony would find his
way easily into Bill Wood's office, as often as three
and four times a week, to throw as many gripes as
he thought Bill Wood was capable of catching.
Many of Tony's textile designs are best sellers. But
why was he such a *constant griper?*

A shapely figure came into Bill's view; it was
Grace Carter, who was joining Doris for a fourth
doughnut. Bill couldn't hear what Grace was asking
Doris, but he could make a guess. Grace, a key-
punch operator for three years, was the unofficial
money collector for employees getting married,
leaving the company, taking off for Europe, re-
cuperating from childbirth, celebrating a fifth anniversary, becoming engaged, entering the military

service, or earning a promotion. Gracie could whip up a collection for almost any reason. Not a very popular girl, pondered Bill, in spite of the shapely figure. Bill made a mental note to see his uncle the next morning on a collection-policy decision, but why, he wondered in the meantime, why was Grace such a *gift collector?*

To the left of the baseball diamond was a quiet pond. Its only disturbance that afternoon was the skimming of pebbles—tossed in measured feet, in measured time, by Pierce. Randy Pierce, the quiet one, was probably the least-known employee to Bill Wood or any other Wood employee. Pierce was alone, kneeling at the pond's edge. Strange, thought Bill Wood, that Pierce seems to be now as he is most of the time on the job. What was he thinking? Did anyone know? Was he happy with the company? Did he like other employees? As Pierce continued to throw pebbles into the water, Bill continued to wonder what made Pierce such a *silent employee?*

Across the pond, Bill saw Keith perched on a large rock, immobile because his arm was in a sling. Ordinarily, Keith would be playing ball, but for two weeks now he'd been off the job. His bandaged arm was the most recent result in a series of accidents for which Keith had become famous. "Look out, Keith!" "Easy, Keith!" "Watch your back, Keith!" These were expressions heard along the corridors each day at Wood's. Keith kept the company nurse busy with frequent bandage changes for toes, fingers, head, and knees. Why, asked Bill Wood, was Keith so *accident-prone?*

Angelo Pavone was the Valentino of Wood and Company, Inc. His Roman features and ironclad muscles provided the stimulus for many of the feminine giggles which surrounded him most of the time. Ange had a way with women. He also had a way with passing the buck whenever an unexpected job came up or when some errors were uncovered. Above the girlish laughter, Bill Wood could hear the echoes of the refrains made popular by Ange: "I really don't know anything about it. Ask Jerry!" "When the bolts came to me, they seemed to be okay, but then Marty took over, and I don't know what went wrong!" "Ask Thompson, he knows more about it than me!" Yep, Bill Wood thought with a smile, Ange is a real smooth operator, but why is he such a *buck passer?*

Bill Wood seemed to be enjoying this view from the oak. He lit a cigarette and thought about how difficult it was for him to understand all these people. He looked around again. He saw and could hear Barney Sloan in some rapid-fire conversation about the way "Some people just don't seem to be able to get the work out in some departments." Bill didn't have to think too long to realize to whom

Sloan's comments were directed. BS, as Sloan was known, was always arguing with someone, usually his boss. In the last five years at Wood, he had been transferred three times, each time at the request of his superior. It looks as if there'll be a fourth time, sighed Bill. How would another company handle Sloan? How many transfers would there be? What made Sloan such a *boss hater?*

The ball game was won by the sales department against the accounting men. Some tidy employees policed the area of empty beer cans, sandwich wrappings, and crumpled white paper cups. Many of the girls were already in line alongside the busses, tired and happy. Before the busses finally left the picnic grounds, Bill Wood also thought about the work shirker, the pay griper, and the grapeviner. He had given thought to the mental caser, the leave-me-aloner, and the antagonizer. Problem employees? Yes, and Wood and Company, Inc. had them. But then, didn't all companies have them? Bill Wood, soon to be in control of this organization, realized that problem employees were as much a part of the firm as a sale, an inventory, or a promotion. That afternoon, he came face to face with the fact that every supervisor, manager, and department head faces employee resistance of some description; obvious or not, it is there. It may take shape in the form of the quiet one or the loud buck passer. Some employees will oppose,

resist, question, and refuse; others will be late, absent,
drunk, and misunderstood.

There are certain things that can be done to help overcome these employee problems, but before getting at
that, let's see why some of our employees are problems,
why they don't get on the band wagon and get the job
done quickly and easily.

### Some employees are problems because—

Men have been emancipated in a variety of ways, but
most men are yet to be freed from fear. Many employees are simply afraid to agree. If it were possible to pene-
trate their thoughts as fear takes hold, we would be apt
to hear a phrase similar to "Why should I stick my neck
out to help that one?" A fearful employee usually doubts
the value of a supervisor's suggestion, fearing that the
advantage is weighted for the supervisor and that he may
regret having agreed. There is satisfaction in the *status
quo* for many employees, and a new suggestion may
bring about a change which may be threatening to the
day-by-day living in which the employee has found peace,
happiness, and security. As many people are afraid of
the future, their reactions on the job usually are in
some form of objection.

As fear is natural in human behavior, so is an underlying resistance to changing a way of life. How often
have you heard these familiar phrases: "What a rut he's

in," or "I like things the way they are," or "Why do they always have to change things around here?" Day in and day out, people like the habits they have patterned for themselves. For some, the coffee break must come at ten in the morning or the world's all wrong; for others a walk around the block in sunshine, rain, or sleet is essential to the proper digestion of a tuna-fish-salad sandwich. Some employees actually integrate resistance patterns into their daily behavior; this is their rut, and they prefer to stay in it. Is there a supervisor, manager, or department head not familar with the employee who can always see a reason for *not* doing something in the suggested way?

Some employees feel it necessary to be always *en garde*, mentally carrying the rapier of jealousy. These employees are resentful toward others on account of known, suspected, or imagined rivalry. We are all aware of what can happen to two people who vie for the same promotion; if it's not around us on the job, we can see it on television, hear about it in a radio drama, read it in a book, see it on the stage, or hear about it in detail from our next-door neighbor. A jealous employee will refuse with no reason, resist any reason, and object to all reasons.

Many employees do not know enough about their needs on the job, or off the job as a matter of fact, but they seek ways to satisfy the needs they know so little about. In this uninformed state of mind, such employees

can't see where they fit in. Needless to say, he who can't
see where he fits in develops into the problem employee. A superior who meets resistance while explaining a new plan to an employee may not have fully fitted
him into the new plan. Ignorance and problems usually
go hand in hand. An employee may act strangely when
he feels he doesn't fit in; if his ignorance is based on in-
correct or untrue facts, expect still stranger behavior.

The employee mold is cast before he reports to work.
This has been done by mother, father, sister, brother,
preacher, priest, teacher, friend. When he's at work, the
mold may get additional rubbing from union steward
and fellow employee. Any of these sources can contribute an idea, a philosophy, or a conclusion which may be
in direct opposition to what the supervisor or manager
wants to get across to his employee. In spite of careful
screening techniques prior to employment, it is not possible to discover the complete make-up of an individual.
Time, money, and pressures on the job these days simply do not permit this. Organizations utilizing the most
modern employment techniques and even those with
psychological and psychiatric staffs know that among
their employee ranks thrive a number of problem employees, many of whom are not yet known to be problem employees but have a problem potential that is apt to
rear its ugly head at the slightest provocation. And not
all these problem-potential employees fall into the cat-
egory of the three A's—the absentees, the accident-prone,

and the alcoholics—even if these are usually the three most noticeable, and often the more easily measurable ones.

Another important reason why employees become problems has to do with the inherent nature of our modern industrial society. The machines, methods, and products in today's society are complex, and often the individual employee's contribution to them is minimal. The employee may consider his role to be unmeaningful, dull, and unsatisfying. His job duty is so simplified that he feels it's only a matter of days before a machine will be invented to take over his work. He wonders if this is upgrading and may conclude that, rather, his contribution is constantly being downgraded and, he thinks, what difference does *he* make in the whole scheme of things? So he punches holes in pieces of metal? So he punches holes in hundreds of cards?

These reasons, then, offer some explanation as to why employees don't always behave on the job in ways we think they should. Fear and jealousy, in many shapes and forms, continue to be basic in human nature. Most people, consciously and subconsciously, want things to stay as they are. Most people have difficulty in understanding their needs, and this vein of ignorance accounts for much misunderstood behavior. People have preconceived ideas and attitudes before one ever meets them; these ideas and attitudes do not always coincide with the demands of the job, the supervisor, or the company.

And man's reaction to the seemingly isolated cogs of the modern industrial process runs a serious parallel to Charlie Chaplin's tribulations in the world-famous movie *Modern Times.*

## A will and a way

Reliable sources claim that one out of every four or five employees is a potential problem. In recent years, studies have estimated the cost of absenteeism to run well over ten billion dollars a year, the cost in human lives lost because of accidents well over ten thousand, and alcoholism has been appropriately labeled in industry as a "billion-dollar hangover." Leaders in business and industry today are well aware of the humane reasons for being concerned about problem employees; as efficient and cost-conscious leaders, they are also concerned about the practical economics which go side by side with problem employees. If the problem has not been nipped in the employment process and blossoms years later on the job, it often makes dollar sense to solve the problem rather than resort to a more costly pattern of a quick Friday-afternoon dismissal. A well-trained employee, with years of company background, is not easy to replace. Then, too, who knows for sure that the replacement will not be problematical? This is why, a few pages back, it was said that the problem employee is an inevitable occurrence for those men and women responsible for the human resources in an organization. Is there anything we can do about this? Let's look at three aspects of coping with it: (1) the role of counseling in helping problem employees, (2) specific steps to be taken with the three A's—the absentee, the accident-prone, and the alcoholic, and (3) ways to overcome the three Rs—refusals, resistance, and rebuttals. Although the following considerations will not solve all your problems, they may help conserve your time, ease your burden, reduce your costs, flavor your morale, and smooth your supervision.

### Counseling

Counseling in business and industrial situations is a relatively new approach in helping the problem employee toward better adjustment. In the counseling process, the employee is made to feel that you are concerned with his problem, that you are trying to help him rather than get rid of him. After the employee *believes* that your desire to help him is sincere, you then provide him with every opportunity to help himself. The quiet atmosphere and the necessary rapport to be established in an interview is especially important when counseling. The big difference between the employment and the counseling interview is that in the latter there is no sense of cross-examination. Unlike the disciplinary session with an employee, there is no expression of reprimand. Cross-examining and reprimanding will not only cancel the effect of the counseling interview but it may add a new dimension to an already existing problem.

To put it in its simplest form, the counseling interview will be of greatest help to the counselor and the troubled employee only if the counselor—

• Gives the employee an opportunity to open up and lead himself into a subject that is uppermost in his mind.

• Listens attentively to what the employee has to say without interruptions from the counselor, which might so easily cause the employee to alter his conversation.

• Gives a wide range of interpretation to what the employee has to say, not in words alone, but for the real thought and meaning that may be beneath and behind the words of the employee.

• Keeps from playing God and judge, behavior critic, or free adviser on any aspect of the employee's problem.

• Keeps from arguing with the employee during the counseling interview.

• Identifies troubled employees early to avoid too many time-consuming counseling interviews.

• Provides a minimum of a half hour for a counseling interview, as nothing much can be gained in less time.

• Gives serious thought to the scope and nature of the employee's trouble in order to decide if his counseling will provide the answer or whether professional help is required.

• Recognizes why the counseling is taking place and what it means to the counselor and the employee.

Counseling employees is an important management tool. Often, it is misunderstood. The important thing to remember is that the counseling interview provides an ideal situation in which the employee can get things off his mind, and it will save him—and you too—from doing so on the job. Equally important is the fact that, when properly handled, the counseling interview will build the employee's confidence in the counselor. This in itself may eradicate the problem the employee has been harboring for months. Don't expect miracles, but if you know a supervisor or a manager who has a department with no problem employees, try to find out whether or not he has taken advantage of sound, intelligent employee-counseling interviews.

### Aiding the three A's

*The absentees.* Personnel and psychological literature generally substantiates the theory that the employee who is chronically absent from work is also a chronic mental case. At this point, Bill Wood of Wood and Company, Inc., may not know the reason why Doris, the chronic sick-leaver, is always absent, but there are at least three things he could suggest to Doris's supervisor, and to himself as heir-apparent, in order to reduce the amount of her absenteeism. It won't be easy, for people like Doris usually feel that the reality of work is so unbearable that the only way they can actually escape from reality is to be absent from work. And this might well be the reason why Grace Carter, the gift collector, spent more time gift-collecting than she spent at her desk.

One immediate way to help reduce absenteeism is to

have some definite rules about it. A formal company sick-leave policy is not sufficient unless the policy describes a procedure for handling excessive absenteeism. The majority of employees may not be aware of management's intention in providing a sick-leave policy, and many will think that it is another form of paid vacation, to be taken whenever he or she wishes additional paid time off. Broad policy statements do not spell out the purpose of a policy in detail; often its language is not understood by the Dorises of an organization. In such cases, the immediate supervisor must spell out the intent of the policy and the possible disciplinary actions that may have to be taken when such a policy is abused. Doris was known for taking Mondays and Fridays off almost every week. Perhaps her supervisor felt she had "the time coming to her"; perhaps he misunderstood the policy and manufactured his own interpretations of it. The establishment of ground rules will combat absenteeism on the front lines.

A second way to keep absenteeism on the firing line is to be sure that consistent disciplinary action is taken with each and every offender. There is nothing more vexing to employees than seeing someone dismissed for three or four absences in a month while another employee continues on the job with a record of ten or fifteen in the same period. Some managers will reprimand one employee for excessive absences and bypass another more serious violator. When the ground rules have been laid, consistency in administering them is essential.

Although a third method in reducing absenteeism may

be more difficult than the first two, it can often result in more satisfactory results. The third method is getting at the *reasons* for the chronic absenteeism; it will require counseling interviews. In counseling, the counselor must be careful to avoid a feeling on the part of the employee that he is being reprimanded for being absent. All aspects of the job and its environment should be explored, as the underlying reason for the absence may be buried somewhere there. It will be important to discuss the employee's associates, his working conditions, his ability to perform the required duties, his understanding of the work to be done, and what his reactions may be to any one of these. If the counselor can isolate one or more reasons for the absenteeism, he will then know the area of discontent on the part of the employee, and this may be the very thing he can easily correct. And in so doing, he can correct the absenteeism along with it. The sore spot uncovered in a counseling interview may be the reason for absenteeism of other employees, as well. Their absenteeism may be reduced by correcting the particular cause of one employee's complaint.

In some severe cases of no-show, the only answer may be professional help or dismissal. When dismissal is effected, and for good reason, such disciplinary action on the part of a manager or company is generally understood and accepted by most employees, especially by the chronic workers.

*The accident-prone.* Safety experts claim that employees who experience numerous accidents at work are not crossing paths with black cats—that, rather than attribute injury after injury to bad luck, it would be revealing to look into the mental disturbances of these employees. In the Du Pont organization, where safety records come off on top, Gerald Gordon has written, after much study which couples accident proneness with mental illness, that the core of the employee's problem in this respect is his failure as a whole person. He further explains that the employee who is a potential accident victim is often well trained for his job and has a long service record but tends to evade the rules of working and of living, and that he is frequently the victim of his own emotions, which he bottles up and then turns against himself. According to Dr. Gordon and other authorities, accident-prone employees can be helped if they are discovered early enough and something is done to help them. These authorities have suggested psychiatric help, but this is not always possible, nor is it always desirable.

Since a supervisor is not usually equipped to provide psychiatric help, there is one simple way for him to reduce accidents: by using the authority that has been put in his hands to see to it that all employees follow established safety rules and practices. See that workers are wearing their hard hats or helmets when blasting the side of a hill; in carrying pipe, hard-toe safety shoes are surely required—don't let soft shoes get into the act; grinding operations require safety goggles—are all eyes protected?

There's no room for leniency when it comes to safety rules and practices. Don't spoil the accident-prone employee. Don't pamper him. This is one place where each supervisor should use the full range of his authority. In this way, accidents will be reduced to a minimum, if not completely eliminated.

*The alcoholic.* Ted Thompson, Wood and Company's Mr. Moonshine, would never admit that liquor was out of his control. On the day of the picnic, one could hear him say that he could take it or could push it away. Others would say that he couldn't admit to himself that he no longer had the ability to control the amount of alcohol he consumed. Ted was a problem Bill Wood would have to face soon. On his way back from the picnic that Sunday, Bill had some pretty good ideas about this. He knew that, whatever he attempted to do, he would have to move slowly and cautiously. Bill's company had no program to aid alcoholics, nor did it have a psychiatrist on its staff. There was the company doctor, however. And better still, there was a branch of Alcoholics Anonymous in their city.

Bill and Ted were on excellent terms. They liked each other, and Bill knew that Ted had respect for him and confidence in him. Bill made up his mind that he would have a heart-to-heart talk with Ted, hoping that he could persuade Ted to talk to the company doctor, who in turn would advise him to look into Alcoholics Anonymous. Bill knew that AA had a record of many successes in helping alcoholics, and this could be hope for Ted. Simple? No, not at all. But whether Ted would admit it or not, he was an alcoholic. His sales for the company were good when he was on the job, but his general pattern was poor attendance, sporadic sales, frequent distasteful behavior, and general lack of respect for company policies and practices. If Ted was not willing to get hold of himself, dismissal in a short period of time would have to take place. Bill Wood saw this coming. The most effective way to handle an alcoholic is to see that he is referred to the company doctor, who should see to it that the alcoholic is referred to a psychiatrist, to a special clinic for alcoholics, or to Alcoholics Anonymous. The alcoholic requires professional help; the supervisor should help him get it. Bill Wood knew this was what he had to do.

## Reducing the three Rs

Experienced managers of people know that all employees cannot be handled in the same way; the differences in employees' personalities usually dictate a variety of actions for the manager. Some employees want to be told exactly what to do, others what not to do; some need coaxing; some want time to think things over; some will agree easily, and others will never agree.

If the manager understands individual employee personalities, he can adapt his approach, each time he needs to, in getting them to cooperate, see his point of view.

and get a job done. Bill Wood, picnicking under the big oak, began to see some of the Wood employees in a different light. On that warm Sunday afternoon, he identified a number of Wood problems. On his way home from the picnic he knew what he would do about some of them. He had plans for Ted, the alcoholic, and Doris, the absentee. But what about Tony, the constant griper? Randy Pierce, the silent, resentful one? Angelo, the buck passer? And Sloan, the boss hater? These men, thought Bill Wood, had many years of service and had done some good work for the company, but they made many difficult hours for their superiors by refusing to accept new ideas, by resenting certain company policies, and by providing rebuttals to many supervisory requests.

For a moment, Bill Wood caught hold of himself. He knew that some employee resistance was a good thing for the company. He knew that, at times employees actually were encouraged to voice their objections to the way things are being run. Last year's morale survey was a worthwhile project, thought Bill. Many of the objections and gripes were turned into real assets for Bill and his uncle—the negative factors revealed by some griping employees actually provided guidance for some areas of their operations which might have gone otherwise unnoticed and neglected. And, too, thought Bill, some employees have an honest desire to help correct things; though they object and resist, their interest in the company is sincere. Bill began to feel that some resentment from employees should be greeted with open arms, for this in itself was one way to "get closer to employees," to have them know that everyone is on the same team. It would be a dull outfit if all employees adopted a "What the h . . l" attitude and looked in another direction every time something new was announced. It was easy for Bill to recall the tons of rationalizations heaped on the managerial force, day in, day out. He could hear the grumblings from Tony, Angelo, and Sloan:

"I don't care what happens around here."

"Well, let's see what happens about it later."

"These guys want blood from a stone."

"My leg is killing me. I can't help out now."

"She must think I own half the company."

"I just don't see how that's going to work."

"Why does he always pick on me?"

Evasive excuses or real resistance are basic with the problem employee. Although excuses may not always be serious, real resentment from an employee will usually prevent agreement. Refusals to do a certain job, resentment of a supervisory suggestion, or rebuttals to a new method—all have to be dealt with in some manner. "How can this be done?" queries Bill Wood. What would he say to Tony, the constant griper, the next time he pushed his way into Bill's office bubbling over with "Why in the world do we need this darned new form?" If only there were a simple way of handling this problem employee, this resentful guy, this nagging textile designer. There is no simple way, concluded Bill. But Bill had given a lot of thought to many of the Wood "people problems." At home, that evening, he stayed up late putting on paper some ideas that could be used to prevent or at least reduce the backbreaking, cost-building, work-hampering habits and attitudes of a score of resentful Wood employees. Bill worked out a series of practical suggestions that could be used by supervisors, managers, and department heads in solving some of the problems they were having with some of their problem employees.

*"Let's take a look at both ideas."* Many employees will meet supervisory ideas with a counteridea, often conjuring the alternative proposal on the spur of the moment. Of course, your idea has been carefully worked out by you or your superiors and, therefore, should stand a good test of comparison with other suggestions. A point-by-point comparison of both ideas at hand, spelling out the pros and cons of each, may satisfy a resentful employee that what is being proposed by you is, in the long run, the better of the suggestions.

An important point here is that the employee has been heard, and often this in itself will erase the resentful attitude he worked up on the spur of the moment.

*"Look, let me show you how it works."* Most employees like to hear, feel, see, smell, and touch things themselves before they are convinced of the validity of a new

idea or suggestion. The mere act of demonstrating a new method, a new machine, or a new process will help in getting the idea across. Just as a gas-appliance salesman will say to a prospective buyer, "Here, try this easy-swinging oven door yourself," so may the manager demonstrate to the objecting employee *the way something works*. In this way, the employee sees, hears, feels, touches, and smells for himself, and perhaps the problem he posed may solve itself.

*"Remember Mae Higgins? She didn't like the new files, but she...."* Citing the experiences of other employees, supervisors, and companies will often prove a point. Explaining the objections that Mae Higgins had at one time to a new filing system, or whatever it might have been, and then pointing up her adjustment to it and eventual acceptance of it will do a great deal in encouraging the employee to take another look at the suggestion. If the case you cite is the right one, the objecting employee will be inspired along new directions and may cast aside his rebuttal of what you proposed.

*"Try it for two months—you can always come back to your old job."* Some reassurance from you will alleviate an employee's fear of change. Even though you have come up with all the sound reasons in the world why, for example, Pete should be promoted to a higher-rated job, Pete himself may not have the immediate confidence in himself that he is able to perform well in the new assignment. Assuring him of a specified trial period in the new

venture, whatever its nature may be, will give him additional confidence. Take care in the way you phrase
these assurances, as they could, improperly worded, add
to already existing antagonism or fear.

*"Sure, Tony, what you say is true, but...."* There are
times when the resistance you meet will be valid, when
it will be almost impossible to remove. At such a time,
you will have to counterbalance it. For example, one day
Tony got to Bill Wood's office with the gripe that Textiles, Inc., had two more paid holidays than Wood and
Company gave their employees. There was no point in
wasting time arguing about this. Bill knew this to be
a fact. If Tony came in again with this gripe, Bill might
now say, "Sure, Tony, what you say is true, but have you
compared the vacation policies? At Textiles, Inc., you
don't get three weeks vacation until you've been on the
payroll for twelve years. Here at Wood, we get three
weeks after ten years."

*"I really don't know, Angelo, but let me see what I
can find out."* Angelo's buck passing usually put his boss
on the spot. Angelo would usually try clever questions
in order to distract from the task at hand; he enjoyed
"stumping the boss" and "getting someone else to do that
little extra job." Angelo's supervisor would have to learn
that one way to deal with Angelo would be to admit that
he didn't know the answer to Ange's question, but that
he would take concrete steps to find out. This would
show Angelo that his boss took him seriously and wasn't
bluffing, and when the answers were given, Angelo would

realize how foolish he was to have asked the questions in the first place. In time, Angelo might learn that respect for an honest boss was deserved.

*"I know things have been rough for you, Randy—why don't you tell me about it?"* Many silent employees are resentful. Until this resentment can come out in the open, there is little chance for agreement between supervisor and subordinate. So was the case with Randy Pierce, the silent one who pitched pebbles at the company picnic. Behind a wall of silence, Randy said nothing, asked nothing. Who knew whether Randy had been wronged, treated unfairly? But, then, who ever took time to find out what Randy was really thinking? Bill Wood, if he were Randy's superior, would now be sympathetic to Randy's feelings. He would provide a situation wherein he would ask, "Why don't you tell me about it?"

*"You probably forgot, Grace, but we have a memo. . . ."* Some problem employees forget the rules by which all work in an organization. Often, at orientation time, a new employee is handed several booklets for his guidance in getting along on the job. But these pamphlets, booklets, and brochures are misplaced or buried in a bottom drawer at home. Or, in some companies, rules are unwritten. There may not be a statement in writing about latenesses, for example, or the supervisor may not have taken time to spell out the rule to employees when they were first employed. Many supervisors and managers resort to off-the-cuff sarcasm regarding employee behavior. A resounding crack such as "Who told you to

come in late?" will only cause an emotional upheaval in the rule-breaking employee. Some superiors feel that it is their responsibility to let all their subordinates know that "they are not getting away with a thing," and the actions of such superiors will upset and irritate employees. Diplomacy and tact are essential in the proper handling of all problem employees. As for Grace, the gift collector, her supervisor should talk to her and start in this way: "You probably forgot, Grace, or perhaps I forgot to mention it to you, but we have a memo from upstairs which asks us not to collect money from anyone outside our department, whatever the reason may be. Don't you think in the future you. . . ."

*"You can't afford not to, Joe."* Most employees who refuse, resist, or rebut usually have at tongue-tip an excuse for not doing something. Their excuses run along these lines: "I would really like to, but I simply can't afford to," or "I know that would help me, but I haven't the time," or "No one else seems to be doing anything about it, so why should I?"

If there is a sound reason for the supervisory suggestion, and there usually is, the supervisor should be prepared to explain why an employee can't afford *not* to follow through on the suggestion, or why it will pay him to find the time. This should not be too difficult to accomplish. For example, attendance at a two-hour course, six weeks running, will result in improved performance on the part of the employee; better training of employees will improve productivity and reduce turnover; better performance leading to a promotion will mean more money for the wife and kids; a good attendance record means a better chance for a merit increase; careless work habits resulting in serious accidents could mean weeks at no pay; overtime means extra money for extra comfort; helping someone today will mean getting help from that someone tomorrow, and working in this way will bring added enjoyment to the work.

## The climate counts

In managing your human resources, you affect the behavior of your employees, consciously or unconsciously. You work, strive, and hope that training them makes them do a better job, that new procedures and policies are understood and accepted, and that cooperation on the job comes willingly.

In managing the problem employee, these hopes are more difficult to fulfill. Yet, you know that your company must show a profit for the goods it produces or the services it renders in order to provide wages for employees and returns for stockholders. You know that such profitable production depends on the cooperation of capital, management, and labor. To achieve this, you know that your employees must be willing to do their share, must be regularly on the job, must have the capacity to work as members of a team, that accidents must be reduced, errors eliminated, and psychological conflicts minimized.

The climate you create for such conditions to hold for

your employees is extremely important. This climate was succinctly described by William C. Menninger and Harry Levinson,* both with the Menninger Foundation, who wrote that the employee must find in his work:

1. A sense of shaping his own life activities.
2. A sense of participation with dignity both in the task and in the decisions relating to it which affect him.
3. A sense of status, of worthwhileness, of recognition.
4. A sense of creative contribution—of giving something of himself for the betterment of his fellows.

But what about you—the foreman, the supervisor, the manager, the department head, the executive? Is it not your job to create positive psychological climates and reduce or eliminate negative conditions? Is it not basic in managing your human resources that you, yourself, develop an understanding of human motivation and psychology?

Isn't it true that he who manages human resources must create positive psychological conditions for himself? Should he not seek counsel and guidance to better understand his own psychological conflicts? Should he not seek advice and direction to better deal with the specific psychological burdens of his job? And shouldn't he be wise enough to institute the same kinds of measures for those who make up his employee group?

How many supervisors and managers do you know

---

* "Psychiatry in Industry," *AMA Personnel*, September, 1955.

who each morning start out on an ulcerous day? How many TV commercials offer the busy executive relief with "sufferin" pills? Hasn't "tranquilizer" become a household word? And do you ever feel you're "living on nerves"? Yes, some employees *are* problems. And so are some bosses. But the supervisor who has learned *what to worry about* and *how to release his anxiety* is more capable of coping with the extra burden of a problem with a problem employee.

AIR

# UNION CONTRACTS

## *a sticky matter of stick-to-itiveness*

Of all professional people, it is quite obvious that men of management have been victims of the poorest public relations. An outstanding example of this is in the area of labor relations. In evaluating management men on integrity, morality, or culture, a majority of public raters seem to use a different yardstick, one they daren't use on educators, historians, musicians, or artists. Despicable

Mr. Scrooge, conceived by Charles Dickens in the middle of the nineteenth century, was a clear example of the selfish entrepreneur. The boss and businessman for many decades have been painted as beady-eyed, long-fingered, and black-coated ogres, out to fleece the public and exploit their employees. Union propagandists have generally characterized the boss as an old sly fox, lurking behind a tree with gnashed teeth, waiting for the kill. This characterization also has penetrated American literature. Dreiser's *The Titan,* Howells's *The Rise of Silas Lapham,* and Serling's play, *Patterns,* are some examples of yesterday's and today's bad men in industry.

Each generation bears an imprint of the previous generation; still with us, ghostly as they may be, are the robber barons of the last century. Whether or not labor organization was an answer to the Jay Goulds or the Jim Fisks is still debatable. In spite of our robber-baron ghosts, members of management now know that a company would not survive unless it passed three stringent tests: (1) It must provide a useful service; (2) it must maintain a high employee morale; and (3) it must keep customers satisfied. It is apparent that our twentieth-century industrial society does not sit alone while taking these tests. On almost every seat is the union partner. For many companies, survival would be limited or perhaps impossible if they did not realize three additional facets which affect their very existence: (1) that organized labor, over the past thirty or forty years, has gained such tremendous power that it can cripple not only a company but a nation; (2) that the entire area of management-labor relations has brought about significant laws by which we must live; and (3) that labor contracts, written for the purpose of preventing labor trouble, must be lived with also.

A prevalent misconception in most companies is that only the president or perhaps a chief counsel is responsible for the management-labor relations and the negotiated labor contract. In union organizations, on the other hand, no such belief exists. From union president to shop steward, every individual in union management is responsible for "managing" union objectives. A quick glance at any of the manuals issued to shop stewards by a variety of unions clearly demonstrates that the union expects from a shop steward just about what management should expect from its foremen, supervisors, department heads, and managers. For example, here are some of the things union management ordinarily directs its shop stewards to do: See that employees get fair treatment according to law; see that grievances are taken to the company supervisor as soon as possible; see that employees understand all implications of the union contract; see that you keep cool, act intelligently, and get along with foremen and supervisors; and so on.

There is no question in the minds of union management men that a well-trained shop steward who is fully aware of the techniques required to obtain a proper adjustment to a grievance, who knows the ins and outs of the grievance procedure, and who is cognizant of his responsibilities in the administration of the union contract is worth his weight in gold. In industrial circles, one hears over and over again the familiar phrase whispered by management men: "The union is here to stay." But one wonders if these same men realize the full implications of such a statement? Are they aware of the real potentiality that the unions possess in making or breaking their organizations? Are they aware of the Simon Legree images that the ordinary worker has of them? Are they aware of what they can do to erase this erroneous picture? Do they understand their management responsibility in working with the labor contract—that what they do with it will determine better or poorer boss-employee relations? Do they know that, though the top official's signature is on the contract, he has signed in behalf of all his administrators?

These questions, then, bring us to the core of this chapter.

One way of creating harmonious company-union relations is by effective contract administration. Industrial and business leaders must increase the awareness of responsibility in administration of the contract for those individuals who handle the contract on a day-to-day basis. The contract is one instrument which can be used to make coherent relations between the company, its employees, and its union. If company administrators fail to take an interest in it, areas of conflict are bound to arise. If your employees are unionized, you should live by the articles in the following agreement which has been written especially for you. Although this agreement was made and entered into yesterday, it should be put into effective administration as of today.

### Agreement between the Company President and All Levels of Management

*(including the Section Head,.Leadman, Foreman, Supervisor, Department Head, Superintendent, Manager, etc.)*

WITNESSETH:

Whereas the company is engaged in the manufacture of essential goods which vitally affect the health, safety, and well-being of a considerable part of the population of the country, all members of management, regardless of the level on which they administer company policy, shall be responsible for effective contract administration in order to avoid (1) any interruption of the company's services to the public, (2) any harm to the full employment and well-being of all employees, and (3) any decrease in the continued expansion of the company's business.

### article i: Contract Administration

Each member of management [and this includes the Supervisor—Auditing Department where 8 auditors and 29 various clerks are gainfully employed in Maystown, Indiana] must understand the company philosophy that each management member is responsible for the day-to-day administration of the labor contract; that it must be administered fairly and impartially and be built on this most important principle: the best labor-management results will be obtained only if the relationship between the employee and his immediate superior is direct, clear and authoritative; that this relationship should be healthy and need not be jeopardized by the presence of a shop steward; that each member of management should know his employees and in this way only can he know and understand their needs, desires and problems.

### ARTICLE II: SPIRIT OF NEGOTIATIONS

Each member of management [and this includes the Service Manager who supervises 37 air-conditioning servicemen in Los Alamos, California] must understand that although he does not occupy a seat at the labor negotiation table, he still has a great deal to do with it. He must be aware of the fact that many of the union demands which are placed on the table have their origin in his day-to-day operation. He must understand the value of keeping written records on the important events that have taken place in his location, including production data, leaves of absence, promotions, layoffs, and any other facts which may be needed at contract negotiation time. That in addition to the above, it is most important that each management member keep the company informed of any situation which *may* have a bearing on any labor relations matter, even if they occur outside of his jurisdiction. That in this way, though he is not at the negotiating table in body, he will be there in spirit.

### ARTICLE III: CONTRACT AWARENESS

Each member of management [and this includes the Platform Agent who supervises 14 train conductors and 74 porters in the Doddstown, Michigan, district] must use all his God-given judgment in administering the union contract with the help of his superior who will see to it:

That as a management man he will be given a *real* opportunity to offer suggestions about the contract before it is negotiated. That immediately upon the issuance of the negotiated agreement, he will be instructed on all its major provisions;

That the industrial relations specialists will be available for guidance, advice or interpretation as they are needed;

That if these opportunities are not offered to those immediately responsible for administering the contract, steps will be taken to correct this situation by requesting help.

### ARTICLE IV: CONTRACT ALIVENESS

Each member of management [and this includes the Assistant Foreman who is in charge of 9 mechanics at the Lindenburg Airport, New Jersey] must comply with all provisions of the contract and not allow them to *atrophy*. If action is not taken against certain employees who do not comply with contract provisions, it may be interpreted as if company and union officials had decided to drop these provisions-in-violation from the contract. That although employees pay particular attention to the major provisions such as overtime, seniority, promotions and rates of pay, they may forget or ignore the less significant [to them, anyhow] provisions which cover smoking, coffee breaks, rest periods and wash up time. To keep the contract alive, all provisions will be observed and enforced.

ARTICLE V: BEWARE: PAST PRACTICES

Each member of management [and this includes the Clerical Supervisor at the Local Office in Eastport, Maine] must understand that arbitrators look to past practice in settling many disputes. That it is impossible to completely state the intentions of both parties in the contract, and that in such cases where the contract is not specific, past practices are taken into consideration in settling a dispute. Each member of management should refer to the details of the company's most recent case of arbitration, wherein the arbitrator ruled in favor of the Intermediate Clerk's promotion. In this case, the Clerical Supervisor for years had been promoting on a seniority basis, although this was not covered by contractual agreement. A grievance was filed by the Intermediate Clerk because she was not considered for the promotion to Senior Clerk. The arbitrator proclaimed that it was his obligation to interpret the contract according to the intent of both signees to the agreement and that in this case, it was clear that the Clerical Supervisor had been promoting other employees for years on a seniority basis. Be alert to "past practices" in your daily administration of the union contract.

ARTICLE VI: ADJUSTMENT OF GRIEVANCES

Each member of management [and this includes the Pressroom Supervisor responsible for 11 Offset-Printing Press Operators in the Linkville Plant, South Carolina] must see to it that all grievances are properly disposed of at the first step of the grievance procedure. That it is his responsibility to carefully explore the details of the grievance and refer it to higher levels of management only in unusual cases. That to function as a member of management, he must learn to cope with the problems in connection with grievances and their settlements thereof. Grievances that go beyond step one may be an indication that management men are not properly carrying out their duties. If and when it is necessary to carry a grievance beyond step one, the issues and circumstances of the grievances must be put in writing as soon as the foreman or supervisor and the shop steward have concluded that a reasonable and proper settlement could not be reached. Unless there are circumstances beyond your control, grievances should be handled within reasonable time limits in order to prevent additional grievances on the same subject before the old complaint has been settled and to ensure the least amount of time interference with improved union-management relations.

### ARTICLE VII: SHOP STEWARD COMPATIBILITY

Each member of management [and this includes the District Manager responsible for Meter Repairmen, Automotive Mechanics, Machinist Helpers and Warehousemen at Canesville, Ohio] must see to it that every effort is made to cement relations with the shop steward as he, too, is an employee of our company; however, this does not mean that in so doing, prerogatives as a management member of this organization are forfeited. What this does mean is that time should be taken, interest shown and sincerity displayed when the shop steward wants to discuss a grievance. That the facts relating to the what, why, when, how and where may adjust the grievance before it goes any further. That the job of the shop steward is to represent employees with grievances and that he will fight hard to win his case. That relating the grievance to the contract may indicate that there is no sound basis for the grievance at all. That gathering the facts and delaying the decision until all aspects of the grievance have been carefully considered [and let's be reasonable about the delay here] may clear the way for better relations with this employee, the union steward. Remember, that one way to keep the steward in line is to have him realize that you are just as much concerned as he is with employee problems and their quick solutions.

### ARTICLE VIII: PUTTING YOUR DECISIONS INTO ACTIONS

Each member of management [and this includes the Foreman at the Propane Plant in Midasville, Texas] must understand that there is nothing in our union contract which deprives management of its right to maintain discipline. That in our union contract there is no joint-determination clause. That the disciplinary decisions you make and actions you take do not require you to discuss them with the union steward before you effect them. Discuss such cases with the steward *after* you have effected the decision. Remember that both management and the union have certain prerogatives. As a member of management, you have a right to make a decision. The union steward has a right to protest your decision, but this does not mean that you should not exercise your prerogative to effect it. Beware that you do not set the precedent of joint-determining your rights in disciplinary or in other areas of your operations.

### ARTICLE IX: BEWARE: BEATING THE CONTRACT

Each member of management [and this includes the Building Maintenance Supervisor in charge of Janitors, Porters, Maintenance Men and Gardeners in Couperstown, Georgia] is not to try to "beat the contract" in spite of the fact that they think they are doing the company a favor. Each foreman, supervisor, and manager must be aware of the fact that the negotiated contract was carefully thought out, worked over and agreed to by both parties; that unilateral action by any member of the management organization to construct his own contractual clauses will not be tolerated. Be it known that difficulty was encountered in our Couperstown, Georgia, location because the Building Maintenance Supervisor gave his own interpretation to the following contractual clause in the following way: Contractual clause—Whenever continuous overtime work for two hours or more is required and at intervals of five hours subsequent thereto, the Company shall, for each and every such occurrence, furnish the employee a meal at its own expense and afford the employee an opportunity of eating same, or in lieu of such employee shall be paid the equivalent of one hour's pay at his regular rate. Supervisor's action—Supervisor was dismissing employees several minutes prior to two hours overtime, although additional work needed to be done, in order to save himself the trouble of providing meals to employees (and according to the Supervisor—to save the Company money). Be it known that at the following contract negotiation, three months later, union negotiators pressed for meal provisions at the completion of *one* hour of overtime. As a representative of management, you are *not* to attempt beating the contract. The union contract under which we work took many long hours, many brains and lots of money to negotiate; whether or not you were at the table, you were there in spirit. Don't spoil it by arbitrary and unilateral practices. If you believe that it takes two to tango, your beating the contract is only an invitation for someone else to do likewise.

### ARTICLE X: STEWARD STRATAGEMS

Each member of management [and this includes the Foreman in charge of 4 Telephone Linemen As and 6 Telephone Linemen Bs at LaSalle, Minnesota] must understand that

there are times when union representatives see to it that
grievances are submitted by the gross. This is usually done
for tactical reasons. When this is the case, the careful management man should seek advice from his superior or the
industrial relations staff specialists. And this is the time to
be especially firm. Beware of overzealous arguments from the
union steward in defense of employees; much of the heel
kicking is probably unjustified.

### ARTICLE XI: LABOR LAWS

Each member of management [and this includes the Superintendent in charge of 24 truck drivers at Motor Vehicle
Dispatching Station No. 22, Crestville, Arizona] should be
familiar with the elements of several basic labor laws, as
these laws govern the legal relationships you have with your
employees. That today, labor legislation is a vast comprehen-
sive body of laws and regulations which govern the working
conditions of the worker and the relationship between the
employee and the employer. That this legislation is not
static; it changes and grows as social and economic conditions
vary. The initial labor laws dealt with child labor, then with
shorter hours, workmen's compensation, minimum wages,
employment of women before and after childbirth and anti-
injunction laws.

SECTION 1: *Labor Management Relations Act, known as the
Taft-Hartley Act, passed in 1947*

This Act superseded (amended) the National Labor Relations Act, popularly known as the Wagner Act, of 1935.
The Wagner Act was the first Federal law dealing specifically
and entirely with problems of trade union organization and
collective bargaining activities (not including the railroad
industry).

Be it known that the Taft-Hartley Act defines a Supervisor as:

> The term *supervisor* means any individual having authority, in the interests of the employer, to hire, transfer, suspend, lay off, recall, promote, discharge, assign, reward or discipline other employees, or responsibility to direct them, or to adjust their grievances, or effectively to recommend such action, if in connection with the foregoing the exercise of such authority is not merely routine or clerical nature, but requires the use of independent judgment

That you are legally a representative of the company and are subject to the provisions of the law as are other members of the management team, including myself. That this is made more clear by the fact that according to the law you cannot be considered as an "employee" for purposes of bargaining; that because you act for the employer, you are, in effect, the employer. That this law imposes certain restrictions on your behavior which include the following:

1. Even if an employee asks for advice about union membership, you cannot give any;
2. You cannot discriminate between union and nonunion employees;
3. You cannot ask an employee if he is a union member or whether or not he attends union meetings;
4. You cannot assist the union in any way nor can you pass out union petitions, brochures, pamphlets or other union literature.

That the major provisions of the law deal with the following:

1. The law defines unfair labor practices by both management and labor;
2. The law reaffirms the right of labor to strike;

3. The law defends the principle of negotiating differences between management and labor;

4. The law strives to restrain excesses by both management and labor;

5. The law strives to protect the public against strikes which would be harmful to the national interest; and

6. The law strives to protect the interests of union members by restraining certain actions on the part of unions.

SECTION 2: *Labor Management Reporting and Disclosure Act of 1959 (Labor Reform Act) known as the Landrum-Griffin Bill.*

Be it known that "The new Act assures union members of equal rights within their union, protects them from oppressive disciplinary action by the union, and gives them an adequate remedy to enforce their rights. It accomplishes this by a so-called 'Bill of Rights' that guarantees the following:

1. Equal rights to vote in union elections, nominate candidates, attend meetings and vote on matters before such meetings.

2. Right to assemble with other members and express their views at union meetings; right to express their views on candidates and other subjects.

3. Right to vote on increases in union dues.

4. Right to sue their union or officers in a court or before an administrative agency, appear as witnesses, or petition for legislation, without fear of retaliation by the union.

5. Right to timely notice and a full hearing before being disciplined for any reason other than non-payment of dues, notwithstanding provisions to the contrary in any union's constitutions and by-laws.

6. Right to receive, on request, a copy of any contract the union has with the members' employer." *

The law makes it mandatory for union officials to report any business arrangement they have entered with employers or unions and requires that officials who handle more than $5,000 be bonded. Unions are also forbidden to lend more than $2,000 to any union officer or employee. Anyone with a criminal record is prohibited from holding a union office until five years after his conviction and union election of officers must be made by secret ballot within specified time limits. Be it known further that we, as employers, must file with the Secretary of Labor, reports of payments to unions, union agents, labor relations consultants, employees or employee groups or committees where an attempt is made to influence the employees' choice of representatives.

"Blackmail" or "Recognition" picketing is prohibited under the new Law. Often, where the union's majority status was in question, picketing to force recognition without an election was used. This kind of picketing can no longer be used. "Secondary boycotts" have also been outlawed. An example of this would be where a trucking company driver refuses to transport merchandise to another company which the union is attempting to organize.

Be it known that this piece of legislation primarily deals with organizational disputes and internal union procedures; that most companies whose employees are wholly or partially unionized, and that there are almost 100,000 such companies in this country, are not troubled primarily with these subjects. Rather, according to Theodore W. Kheel, their problems involve collective bargaining as it has developed during

* *Labor Report*, vol. 17, no. 10, Sept. 11, 1959, p. 2, Prentice-Hall, Inc., Englewood Cliffs, N.J.

the past two decades. Mr. Kheel says: "The results of bargaining and contract administration ... affect not only the size of the employer's wage bill but employee productivity as well—deep concerns of practically every company in the country. These problems of collective bargaining are not solved by the new Kennedy-Landrum Law, despite its correction of many abuses. The solution still lies, not in the halls of Congress, but with the companies and unions themselves." *

SECTION 3: *Public Contracts Act, known as the Walsh-Healey Act, passed in 1936.*

Be it known that this law established labor standards on government contracts for materials, supplies and equipment exceeding $10,000. That the basic eight-hour day was set, the forty-hour work week was set, provisions for child labor and requirements for safety and health were set and that the Secretary of Labor could set minimum wage rates.

SECTION 4: *Fair Labor Standards Act, known as the Wage and Hour Law, passed in 1938.*

Be it known that this law applies to employees engaged in interstate commerce or in the production of goods for interstate commerce. This law set a minimum wage of forty cents per hour. In 1955, the minimum was raised to one dollar per hour and as conditions change, this minimum may change also. This law requires overtime pay at one and one-half times the regular rate for all work after 40 hours in any work week. (Overtime pay is not required for work under 40 hours, for work exceeding eight hours per day, for Sunday or holiday work, as such, for time lost through lateness or for overtime worked contrary to explicit and enforced in-

* *Dun's Review and Modern Industry,* October, 1959.

structions.) Further, this law regulates the employment of all persons under 18. However, any state law or other federal law governs if it fixes a higher age. All employment is prohibited for children under age 14. For those under 16, employment in mining and manufacturing is prohibited. This law also states that the time spent by an employee for his own convenience before and after work, such as changing clothes, getting tools, washing up, etc., need not be paid for. The Wage-Hour Law extends a blanket exemption from overtime to some businesses, and individual exemptions to some employees in businesses that are otherwise covered.

SECTION 5: *Welfare and Pension Plans Disclosure Act, passed in 1958*

Be it known that this law requires administrators of welfare or pension benefit plans to provide copies of the description of such plans and their latest annual reports to the U.S. Department of Labor and to make additional copies of this same material available for examination by any participant.

### Addendum

The *modus vivendi* of Americans has always been to get the job done and get it done properly. How else could this nation, years ago, prove that the American system was superior to anything yet known to man? Other lands, some naturally better endowed than our own, all have recognized that the American working force is second to none, that our industrial *esprit de corps* has brought about the highest production records and standard of living in the history of mankind. The American dream came true for many laborers, immigrants, and eighth-grade graduates who by hard work, ambition, and opportunity stepped up and out of the ranks to run their own companies, build new plants in Europe, and win a second world war. In its growth, American industry has had its problems, but always present has been the American gift of cooperative enterprise—people working side by side, united to achieve a common goal. Often, the labor pains have grown severe, and often our working force has split into camps. Tugs of war, hot and cold, have temporarily brought companies, industries, and the nation to the brink of disaster. Some say that much of the violence and bitterness associated with labor disputes is disappearing forever. Others say that all working people are finding out that they *can* settle their differences to better advantage by sitting down and talking it out. It will be best for you to consider taking the lead in establishing a sound cooperative spirit among your employees. And if you work with a union contract, it's doubly important that you remain in the lead. You need no gun shot to start, no written memorandum from the boss, no labor law to tell you. In your job, *you* are the leader of men.

(signed)

*Your President*

This imaginary contract was written by an imaginary company president for real reasons: (1) Each supervisor should realize that he must create an atmosphere which encourages his people to bring their problems to him; (2) he must realize further that *he* is the key man in the employer-employee relationship; and (3) his labor contract is his rule book for day-to-day activities. Your company president put it this way—in your job, *you* are the leader of men.

# YOUR BOSSES

*inside and out*

14

The general's disdain'd
By him one step below, he by the next,
That next by him beneath; so every step,
Exampled by the first pace that is sick
Of his superior, grows to an envious fever
Of pale and bloodless emulation.

Doesn't everyone have bosses? Next to your wife or
your husband, your sons and your daughters, your
mother and your father, the most important people are

**213**

your bosses. Important because they are influential; they determine, in effect, your economic, social, and political way of life. They influence your earnings, your promotions, sometimes the part of the country in which you live; they help shape city, state, and Federal laws; they expand or contract your business and almost always your job. Who are these bosses? They fall into two general classifications: upstairs and outside. The man or woman to whom you report directly is the one upstairs (or around the corner, up the hall, or across the corridor), and the other—the one outside—is your customer, your client, your consumer, the public. Together, they are your bosses. Everyone has them.

### The boss upstairs

Just as your employees, when gathered around the cafeteria lunch table, may refer to you with pin-pointed and sometimes harsh descriptions of you as boss—perhaps you may be known as the paper pusher, the comma corrector, the goof-off golfer, or the tee martooni drinker —you too probably are able to place your superior in a nutshell of description. Whatever you think of your superior, you should be sure of one thing: He needs you. If this were not so, you would not be there. Earlier in this book your job responsibilities were described. They are not easy ones. In short, you must create pleasant and efficient working conditions for your employees. You must see to it that your operations are on schedule

and that you cooperate with other departments so that
company goals may be realized. This is what your boss
expects of you. Get these jobs done, and the boss finds it
easy to increase your pay, keep you in mind for a promotion, back you up with higher levels of management, and
consider you the "indispensable man" on his staff. Meeting these responsibilities is the biggest part of your job,
and if you do, success is at your doorstep. Yet there are
many who in spite of getting the work out feel they are
not on the best side of the boss. You get your work out—
you know the boss can't get along without you. But do
you know what else he needs?

### The boss needs palatable persuasion

One prerogative of the boss is his authority to approve
or disapprove the request of a subordinate. Perhaps only
yesterday you may have had a request turned down. You
may have left the boss's office seething, saying that "Trying to sell that guy anything is like trying to sell him
the Brooklyn Bridge!" What might the *boss* have said
when you left his office? "Every time that guy wants
something, he sure gives me a big argument." Every
supervisor, department head, and manager must be a
salesman of a sort. He sells, for example, ideas, new
work methods, a revised schedule or a personnel trans-
fer. What assurance can he give himself to get the right
answer from the boss? The next time you need to persuade your boss that you need to add another operator

to the work force, make your persuasion palatable by applying these simple dos and don'ts:

*Don't argue*

THE BOSS: Jim, the budget can't take a new person just at this time. We're already overspent by....

YOU: But a new operator just won't cost that much, and I've not spent a penny more than....

You just told the boss he is wrong. On top of it, you've disagreed with his facts and are beginning to turn the meeting into a debating contest. If the boss is wrong, your argumentation throws your request out of proportion and sets up additional barriers to his acceptance of the idea that a new man is needed and that a new man can be afforded. If the boss is right, what is the point of arguing? Another slap across the face! Another time you've erred! One up for you in how to alienate the boss!

*Avoid the "You'll be sorry" song*

THE BOSS: Jim, the budget can't take a new person at this time. We're already overspent by....

YOU (*fumbling your spectacles and pointing your pencil*): You'll be sorry if you can't see this, Greg. The work simply can't get out, and people....

This attitude on the part of the persuader is threatening and foreboding. It often flexes the boss's biceps, and the persuader is bounced right out the door.

*Don't push too hard*

THE BOSS: Jim, the budget....

YOU: Greg, I know right from the start you'll agree with
this. . . .

This push approach opens the way for the boss to say
immediately right from the start that he *doesn't* agree
with what you have to say. And if the boss doesn't come
to immediate disagreement with your point of view, he
immediately sets his mind to work on finding loopholes
in your argument. The boss doesn't want to be pushed
any more than you do. He considers it part of his job to
identify, evaluate, and decide the issues of a serious situation carefully. This may take more time than you think.

*Consider the boss's point of view*

THE BOSS: Jim, the budget can't take a. . . ,
YOU: Greg, we're over, but you can get by if only. . . .

Well, maybe Greg can't get by! He may have received
a lecture that morning from *his* superior on budget control; maybe at this particular time especially the boss's
point of view must be considered. Concern with our
own point of view alone is a cardinal sin in the art of
persuasion. Take time to figure out and understand the
other side. Knowing what's on the other side will help
you plan your approach more intelligently. It will also
enable the boss to feel his side of the story has been heard
and weighed. When this has taken place, the stage is set
for coordinating a plan for the fulfillment of the subordinate's request.

Remember, the boss wants and needs persuasion, but
he prefers it in palatable portions.

### The boss needs to be in the know

If you've ever said about your boss, "I wonder if he knows what the heck's going on," then you should ask yourself, "What have I been doing to keep the boss informed?" (And what you haven't been doing.) In management circles, and on so many employee rating forms, a familiar and often misunderstood question is, "Does the subordinate involve his principal in the day-to-day headaches of his job?" This question connotes that the boss is not to be bothered, regardless of the nature of the ill. As boss, he is to be shielded from the daily goings-on by the same fencing position that a secretary assumes in protecting him from unnecessary (and sometimes necessary) visitors. This protective type loyalty may be so true blue that the boss, at an important meeting, may be absolutely in the dark about a rather important situation. What he doesn't know *will* hurt him.

Many subordinates speak to their bosses through rose-colored megaphones—everything they say comes out rosy, positive, and constructive. This is also known as the "best lip forward" technique. The boss hears "good things" to such a point that he is the last person to find out that 782 workers in the Crestwood plant went out on strike last night at midnight.

Seeing that the boss is in the know is not easy, but it can be done. It means taking time to discover how the boss wants to learn the news of the day, the news of the week. He may prefer a lunch date once a week, daily notes on buck slips, or full reports at staff meetings. Whichever method is used when you have decided *how* to tell the boss, the biggest concern should be about *what* to tell him. Common sense tells each of us that it is an impossibility to tell him everything; he simply doesn't need to know everything—and hasn't time. The difficulty is in drawing a line in the gray area between ordinary and extraordinary events. In drawing this line, you should keep a keen outlook for any mistake that has been made by you or anyone under your jurisdiction which may spell trouble ahead. The chances are that the trouble is heading right in the boss's direction. The mistake can gain missile momentum and explode in the middle of the twelfth floor. One of the boss's functions is to handle many of these errors, and knowing before explosion time that they have occurred will help him do a better job. Early corrective action on his and your part will eliminate your having to undo it completely.

Making decisions is an ordinary and important part of your job. Some decisions, though seemingly routine to you, are not so from the boss's point of view, as he may be directly involved in the decision you make. Since the boss is ultimately responsible for all your decisions, he is entitled to be in the know where the bigger and more important decisions are concerned. He counts on a steady flow of information for reporting to higher levels of management. He should be in the know when you find it difficult to reach that big decision. Decision making which is difficult for you is usually surrounded by unusual circumstances. When this is the case and the boss shows signs of impatience, don't whisper through the megaphone, "I'm working on it, I'm working on it. It'll be ready soon, it'll be ready soon." Your boss needs to know that you're having difficulty with this particular one. It's time for you to lay the facts on the table for him. As your boss, he feels he can help you. *Involve* your superior in this particular headache, as it will prevent him from having one a week or two later. As you understand your job responsibilities and those of your employees, a knowledge of the boss's responsibilities will help you know how, why, where, when, and about what to put the boss in the know.

### The boss needs a double in dollar dimensions

The American businessman, working and operating through the free-enterprise system, is an exponent of thrift, economy, and cost control. Business management has become an American science because of our ability to produce goods and provide services to meet competition anywhere in the world. Every business operation must show profit if it is to survive. Without this profit, no organization could continue to produce goods or provide services, employ people, or pay taxes to city, state, and Federal governments. The historic American way of staying on top, at home and abroad, is by *keeping costs down*. Only a few years ago, when television sets first appeared on the market, price tags were four times as great as they are today. By keeping costs down, everyone enjoys more of the things that add up to a higher standard of living.

Your boss has been delegated a tremendous financial responsibility in getting his job done. You are his double in your job, and the dimension you give to company dollars will be in direct proportion to your success. Costs will have to be kept under strict control if your unit, section, or department is to succeed. These costs cover wages and salaries, equipment, materials, supplies, maintenance, and, of course, taxes. It's an old story that when profits are high, cost control goes down. When this happens, don't wait for your boss, bank, or board of directors to take corrective steps. Keeping costs down should be your daily concern. Your boss needs to know that you are aware of costs. One way to demonstrate this cost-consciousness is to keep an open door for those cost specialists who may be able to help you. Cost accountants, methods analysts, and time-study men can often see a wasteful procedure or neglectful action that may be costly to the company.

Something else you can do is to study the actual operating costs periodically in your own area of responsibility. Cost data exists in all companies in one form or another. Records are kept for overhead expenses. Wherever possible, production records should be kept for all your employees. Keep a close eye on overtime records. You should understand fully the area of wage and salary administration, for in many companies this is the greatest area of expense. You, in your job, are the main controller for most of these costs. If you are recommending salary increases for several of your employees, your boss wants to know that you've cost-considered the recommendation along with other considerations. If you recommend the purchase of another piece of equipment, he wants to know that you've analyzed the cost situation. He wants to be assured that you've studied your costs with those of a similar operation elsewhere in the company. If your costs are up this week or this month, why have they gone up? Will a new piece of machinery reduce costs? How many mistakes are made? How much overtime? What about a new simplified work method? When higher costs go unexplained, have you let the boss in the know? Are your employees aware of costs?

Management people and labor both must work to keep business expenses to a minimum. In this way, all employees can look forward to job security and better wages. Unstable jobs are a sure sign of a company without cost control; frozen salaries are a sure sign of a company with no profits. If you want better boss relations, keep costs down where they belong.

### *The boss needs reports with rhyme and reason*

Somewhere between the extremes of never communicating in writing and of delivering reams of written pro-
posals, suggestions, analyses, and recommendations to
the boss should be the carefully thought-out report. A
report with rhyme, reason, and easy reading for the boss
is required in almost every phase of management. Most
bosses will agree that they need someone who can think
logically on paper. After all, important actions by most
companies have been based on recommendations which
originally appeared in written reports. The report you
submit to your boss today may be on the president's
desk tomorrow. Is it any wonder why better reports can
help better boss relations?

There are several ingredients which go into a good
report: First, set and state your objective. This really
is your title, and it should be so worded as to attract
attention. Brevity is important here, but don't be so
brief that the subject of your report is unclear. The
second ingredient is in the form of an abstract. It en-
ables the reader to acquaint himself quickly with the
problem and the recommended solution. An introduction is your third ingredient, and it should include brief
background information (why a problem exists or how
a problem developed) and pertinent information about
the situation as things stand now (that is, up to the time

of writing the report). It should explain why the report is being written. It's an overture and should set the scene for the fourth ingredient: the body of the report. If you are recommending a new salary structure, you will probably include descriptions of the "present structure," "proposed structure," "present costs," "proposed costs," etc. If you are recommending the purchase of a new duplicating process, you will subhead your descriptions of its cost, equipment, method of duplication, advantages over present method, cost saving, etc. The fifth ingredient is important because it should incite action on the part of the reader. This section of the report is usually called the conclusion. It contains a review of the facts in the body of the report and a clearly stated proposal or recommendation for action. It sounds like a simple recipe. Not exactly. But if you approach the job of report writing with an enthusiastic attitude and include these ingredients, you can develop an important form of managerial communication between you and your boss. (The boss also likes to have reports in on time.)

### The boss needs some of your expressed dissatisfaction

Any subordinate can be a yes man. Any yes man can be easily dispensed with. It has been said that when two people in management always agree, one of them is unnecessary. Whether or not you read the *Wall Street Journal,* one way to better boss relations and to move up the line is to sever the connections wired in the back of your neck which automatically set up the nod of approval every time the boss says something. Most bosses appreciate the employee who sensibly expresses his dissatisfaction, for in that way present methods are improved and new ideas are born. Dissatisfaction, when not associated with the chronic malcontent, can be an asset to the boss and the business. Allen Hewlett, in *Advanced Management,** reported:

> Extensive inquiry into the factors governing human productivity, conducted by the Institute for Social Research at the University of Michigan, has thrown new light on the nature of the gripe. In the absence of serious psychic disturbances, the man who gripes about the work, his boss and his company is better executive material than the man who either has no complaints (and may be emotionally subservient) or keeps them to himself (possibly because he lacks courage to express them). There is evidence that the personality characteristics that dispose a man to expressions of criticism are also the very ones essential to competence.

An old Chinese adage says that a journey of a thousand miles begins with a single step. What single step are you taking in developing better boss relations? Are you selling your boss in the right way, or are you building antagonisms? Are you filling him in on the things he needs to know, or are you keeping him in the dark? Are you

* Allen Hewlett, "Nobody Cares How Tough You Had It," *Advanced Management,* September, 1956, p. 27.

understanding the importance of controlling costs in your operation, or are you on a mad spending spree? Are you submitting sensible reports or deluging him with untimely, unthoughtful, and useless verbiage? Are you yessing him to death, or are you supplying him with constructive, contemplative, and contagious ideas?

### The boss outside

Public good will is essential to company success. Product packages claim "Quality since 1839," while double-page spreads in national magazines picture the home-made heroes responsible for new and exciting products. Television networks broadcast corporate facts on research spending to make life abundantly richer, while the city newspaper prints the other view—that of a three-week old strike in a local plant. Financial grants to colleges and universities are publicized, while legal claims are settled behind closed doors. Today, sound business acumen requires a business organization to take advantage of every opportunity to keep the masses informed of everything that is being done to improve its services, its products, and its employee relationships. Today's questionable hush-hush activity on the part of any corporate enterprise can easily find its way into tomorrow's front page. And the prancing figure of a five-figured dollar-publicity *stunt* man is only a silhouette these days.

Most industrial organizations have come to realize that

good community and public relations cannot be built alone on a series of "best lip forward" advertisements—that, in spite of the impact of a good ad on the mind of the reader, there are more important aspects to be considered in this important area of creating good public relations. What the company sells in the way of service or product, what it charges for this service or product, and the way in which company employees think, feel, and act in and outside the company are more important factors which mold the corporate image. All the publicity in the world cannot change a poor public attitude into a good one if the basic product or service is not a good one. Each of us has seen the customer walk across the picket line when he knew the service or product was the best he could buy. One restaurant in a large city was able to come out on top in spite of its many months of labor strife because its customers knew and had known for years that theirs was the best food in town. Prices charged for the service or product must be kept competitively low. As stated before, this is a major facet in the American formula for success. This is why cost control is a necessary part of every job in the management team. Employees too should understand that higher prices mean fewer jobs, less take-home pay, and greater job insecurity.

But what about you and your employees and this outside boss, the public? Count the number of contacts you have with people outside your company; count the contacts all other employees in the organization have with outsiders, and the sum of influence on public relations is staggering. This is why today the company with the forward look takes time to train its employees in properly handling the interests of clients, consumers, and customers. A corner drugstore philosophy actually creates a corporate image; you and your employees contribute to it, for better or for worse. What people in the community think of your company has a powerful impact on the success or failure of your company's operations. Good opinions and bad ones are expressed in the corner drugstore. Listen one evening on your way home from work, and you will hear the pros and cons, the ifs and buts, the dos and don'ts, about the latest strike, the unsafe conditions which caused a fire, the delay in completing the clover leaf at the Brandywine intersection, the increased rate for electric service, the meager salaries paid or the high turnover at plant X. What you hear is usually not what someone else has had to say on the subject but what the drugstore philosopher himself has to say, in his own words, about the company, its people, and its policies. As any or all of the above may affect the philosopher, he manages to formulate an opinion, largely based on one or more contacts he had yesterday, last week, or last year with members of these various organizations. In all probability, he is an employee of one of these companies, and his philosophical ifs and buts and dos and don'ts become increasingly influential.

Whether your company employs five hundred, five

thousand, or fifty thousand people, their voices, *in toto,* are the basis on which public opinion is formed. This huge force of public opinion is one of your bosses. Treat it with as much care as you do the boss upstairs. Recognize that all your employees—in the barbershop chair, the neighbor's playroom, or in line at the grocery store —talk, talk, talk. What they say, as employees of the company, is taken seriously. And why not? Isn't the information coming straight from the horse's mouth? And isn't it logical for people to assume that they are talking about things from their points of view? But if they are uninformed about a particular matter inside the company, how could they possibly be dishing out the right information outside the company? And think of it, they talk about company policies, products, programs, problems, and people. Don't count on the company magazine or the memorandum from the president's office to do this job for you. When you have the facts and the full understanding of the issue at hand, get it across to your employees. Most employees like to be in the know; they will speak with clear-cut authority on company subjects, with clear-cut confidence if they know they understand and have been given an insight into company policies, products, programs, problems, and people.

Employees, including yourself, who have *direct* contact with the public make an even greater contribution to community relations, for better or for worse. One of the most important contributions to improved public

relations is made by the interest and information given
by the employee in answer to a customer's problem. Is
there anything more damaging to customer good will
than a department-store clerk who says, "We're out
of size 15," and there on the counter is a full box of
size 15s. But what about the clerk who carefully looks
for your requested size and, finding none, calls the stock
room and has the merchandise ready for sale in a matter of minutes?

An interested employee is easily recognizable and
much appreciated. He constitutes one of the simplest
and best ways to create public good will. Ambassadors
are not needed only in foreign service; every employee
should be an ambassador at large for his own comfort
and satisfaction in life, and for the well-being of his
company and other employees and the community in
general. It is not a bit unusual for the company with
good community relations to have many of its problems
solved with the help of local political administrations.
Most companies at one time or another have to solve
matters dealing with building permits, road maintenance, shipping and receiving facilities, and zoning
codes, to mention a few. Local administrators who think
the company has a questionable reputation may make
things tough by postponing decisions, voicing an un-
savory remark, or placing other obstacles in the way,
many of which are time-consuming and costly to the
company's operations.

Most people crave to belong to something, and they crave more to be proud of that to which they belong. The job of getting along with the outside boss depends on how well you and your staff feel they belong to the company and how proud they are of belonging. This can be accomplished without the use of a rose-colored megaphone. What you and your staff carry out over Mrs. Murphy's back-yard fence, down the bar of overflowing beer glasses, or across the green slopes of the golf course will mesh with the public's idea of who you are, what you are, and for whom you work. Only then will the company's annual report, stories in the local newspapers, radio spot announcements, billboard advertisements, and special documentary facts on the nation's television screens have the support of the millions of corner-drugstore philosophers, whenever and wherever they meet.

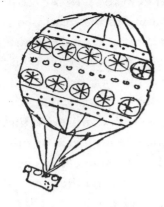

# *15*

# A VIEW

## *a nondimensional affair*

Lao-tse said, "The wise man looks into space and does not regard the small as too little, nor the great as too big; for he knows that there is no limit to dimensions." From this view, we see each human association dependent on the individual's abilities, talents, and acceptance of responsibilities, brought together so that he can live life economically, politically, and socially. Individual development need not be bound by the high walls of corporate enterprise. Conformity of thought, action, and purpose is by no means limited to the large industrial organization; it can be as devastating in the small plant on Elm Street as it can be amidst the tons of concrete and miles of steel in the pulsating avenues of the city. Whoever you be, wherever you are, you have a view.

There is no simple formula for the job which lies ahead. There is no magic pill. No book can provide the specific answers needed for particular problems in this area. But if this book has helped give you one new sense of direction, has provoked some thought on the conventional ways of managing people, and has brought into focus improved ways of working with and through people, then what you see should be encouraging. So why not hitch your wagon to a star? ". . . there is no limit to dimensions."

Milton may have sat on the steps of an English pub in the Cheapside section of London in the early 1600s. His tin cup might have rattled with coins tossed by passers-by. For he, like Homer and Helen Keller, was blind. Their dark victories brought far less dollar satisfaction than the thrill and fulfillment of achievement that each of their lives demonstrated. The twentieth century in these United States has opened more doors of opportunity than ever before. No matter how high the wall, how deep the limitation, only you can reach out to grasp the challenge before you. What could be more challenging than the planning, organization, development, and control of the human resources under your jurisdiction?

# INDEX